Contents

Figures

Managing special needs in the
primary school

Educational management series
Series editor: Cyril Poster

Managing special needs in the primary school

Joan Dean

London and New York

First published 1996
by Routledge
11 New Fetter Lane, London EC4P 4EE

Simultaneously published in the USA and Canada
by Routledge
29 West 35th Street, New York, NY 10001

Typeset in Palatino by
Florencetype Ltd, Stoodleigh, Devon
Printed and bound in Great Britain by
Clays Ltd, St Ives plc

British Library Cataloguing in Publication Data
A catalogue record for this book is available from the British Library

Library of Congress Cataloguing in Publication Data
A catalogue record for this book has been requested

ISBN   0–415–13030–1

Chapter 1

The current situation

When Timothy started at the local village school he seemed to his teacher to be a bright little boy and she had no suspicion of the problems which he would pose later. His older brother Darren had just moved from her class into the next class and was already reading quite well and making satisfactory progress in mathematics. Timothy seemed to settle down quite easily and enjoy all the activities which she was providing. It was only as time went on that she began to realise that he was not making much progress in reading. She tried to make more time to hear him read, which was not easy in a class of thirty-two infants, but the end of the year came and he still had not really started to read at all. He appeared to be unable to remember any words or sounds from one day to the next.

There were only four classes in the school and after discussing Timothy with the headmistress it was decided that he should spend more time in the infant class and that his teacher should try to give him special attention. He still made almost no progress but at the end of his second year he was moved up into the next class. His new teacher was convinced that helping him was mainly a matter of finding things which interested him and accordingly he made books about trains and footballers, copying large passages out of books quite neatly and illustrating them attractively. Unfortunately he was unable to read what he had written or to write very much by himself and his teacher was at a loss what to do next.

Time passed and Timothy gradually moved up the school, still unable to read although his progress was almost normal in mathematics except where reading was involved. The teachers of the top two classes found this even more of a problem than the teachers of the younger children because their training had not prepared them for a child who was still at the beginning stages of reading and writing. They spent time hearing him read but were not really sure how best to help him apart from this.

At one stage the headmistress suggested to his mother, who was concerned about him, that she should help him at home. She blushed deeply and said 'I'm afraid I have the same problem.' Further discussion revealed that there was an older sister in the secondary school who still could not read fluently in spite of the good work of a competent remedial department. Timothy eventually left his village school for the secondary school still unable to read.

This is a true story, although the names have been changed, but it all happened a long time ago when there was very little back-up help for schools and they were left to manage as best they could. It demonstrates how we come to have so many illiterate adults and why we need the Code of Practice to ensure that more is done to deal with the problems of today's Timothys so that no one leaves school unable to read and write and manage the day-to-day mathematics that we all need.

The 1993 Education Act has laid down a number of requirements for the education of children with special needs. The Act defines children with special needs as follows:

A child has a 'learning difficulty' if –
(a) he has a significantly greater difficulty in learning than the majority of children of his age,
(b) he has a disability which either prevents or hinders him from making use of educational facilities of a kind generally provided for children of his age in schools within the area of the local education authority, or
(c) he is under the age of five years and is, or would be, if special educational provision were not made for him, likely to fall within paragraph (a) or (b) when over that age.

(DFE 1993: para. 156.2, p.101)

It points out that children whose mother tongue is not English do not come into the category of having special educational needs.

The Act goes on to make the point that children with special needs should be educated in a school which is not a special school unless this is incompatible with the wishes of their parents. It specifies that when children with special educational needs are educated in other than a special school it must be possible for them to receive the necessary special provision without affecting the provision of efficient education for other children or the efficient use of resources.

The Act requires the governing body to see that children with special needs are adequately catered for and that teachers are aware of the importance of identifying and providing for children with special needs.

The Act is complemented by the Code of Practice on the Identification and Assessment of Special Educational Needs (DFE 1994c) which sets out how schools and Local Education Authorities (LEAs) should implement the Act.

THE DEVELOPMENT OF PROVISION FOR
SPECIAL NEEDS

The 1993 Act and the Code of Practice are the latest developments in a move towards integrating children with special needs into normal schools which has been taking place gradually since the Warnock Report and the 1981 Education Act, both of which recommended a move towards integration. They reflect a general move towards integrating people with disabilities into normal society.

The Warnock Report (DES 1978) estimated that up to one in five children were likely to need special provision at some point in their school lives and this is confirmed in the Code of Practice (DFE 1994c) which also states that:

> only in a minority of cases – nationally around two per cent of children – will a child have special educational needs of a severity or complexity which requires the LEA to determine and arrange the special educational provision for the child by means of a statutory statement of special educational needs.
>
> (DFE 1994c: para. 2.2, p.5)

The conclusion that around 20 per cent of children will have special educational needs at some stage in their school lives means that in a class of thirty children, six may need special provision over the course of their schooling. It can therefore be seen that every teacher and every school will encounter some children who need special provision whether or not children who would formerly have been in special schools are integrated into mainstream schools.

One category of children who might be held to have special needs which was not included in the Warnock Report, nor the 1993 Act or the Code of Practice, is children with exceptional ability. Research (Freeman 1983; Denton and Postlethwaite 1985; and many others) suggests that these children are not extended by their education in many cases and that their needs are not met. This has been a recurring theme in HMI reports from the 1970s onwards. The pressures of the National Curriculum are likely to make it even more difficult for teachers to spend time identifying and providing for these children, yet their needs are considerable and they are important for the future. These children too may need special provision and this book includes them as children with special educational needs.

A whole school approach to special needs is therefore required in which all teachers develop some expertise in dealing with children who have learning problems or who are outstandingly able.

Prior to the publication of the Warnock Report (DES 1978), most of the education of children with disabilities took place in special schools and children were classified according to their particular problems. It was not always easy to do this because a child might have more than one disability. There have also been developments in medicine and health care which have changed the incidence of particular disabilities with consequences for the special schools catering for them.

The Warnock Report (DES 1978) suggested that it might be better to classify children with disabilities according to the way their needs might be met and that where possible such children should be educated in mainstream schools alongside their peer group. These children would be held to have special needs over and above those of the school population generally. The report also stressed the importance of involving parents in considering the needs of a child.

Warnock started with a definition of the goals of education which might be said to apply to the education of all children and not only to those who have special needs:

> First to enlarge a child's knowledge, experience and understanding and thus his awareness of moral values and capacity for enjoyment; and secondly to enable him to enter the world after formal education is over as an active participant in society and a responsible contributor to it, capable of achieving as much independence as possible.
>
> (DES 1978: 5)

The 1993 Act confirmed and brought up to date the arrangements under the 1981 Act for making an assessment of a child's special educational needs, setting out the various stages.

The assessment process involves parents at every stage and they may appeal if they disagree with the final conclusions. Assessment may result in a statement giving details of the child's educational needs, outlining the special provision required and stating the arrangements needed to meet those needs. Once a statement has been issued the child's progress must be reviewed annually.

INTEGRATION

The Code (1994) makes the following statement about integration:

> The needs of most pupils will be met in the mainstream, and without a statutory assessment or statement of special educational needs. Children with special educational needs, including children with statements of special educational needs, should, where appropriate and taking the wishes of their parents into account, be educated alongside their peers in mainstream schools.
>
> (DFE 1994c: para. 2.1, p.2)

The word 'Integration' can have a variety of interpretations. S
et al. (1983) describe the aims of integration as follows: 'Handi<
children should have the opportunity to participate in as many of the
same activities and should be educated in the same manner as their
non-handicapped peers to the greatest extent possible' (p.61).

The Warnock Report (1978) defined three levels of integration:

Locational integration
• where special units are set up in ordinary schools.
• where a special school and an ordinary school share the same site.

Social integration
• where children attending a special class or unit eat, play and
  consort with other children and possibly share organised out-of-
  classroom activities with them.

Functional integration
• where the locational and social association of children with special
  needs with their fellows leads to joint participation in educational
  programmes.

(DES 1978: para. 7.7, p.100)

The Code of Practice suggests that the governing body and the headteacher should determine the school's general policy and approach to
provision for children with special educational needs, establish the
appropriate staffing and funding arrangements and maintain a general
oversight of the school's work.

Integration of children with special needs is not easily achieved. It is
easier if they have been part of the school from the beginning and more
difficult if they have spent time in a special school. Initially teachers, older
pupils and parents will be apprehensive, but eventually everyone comes
to learn the valuable lesson that people with handicaps are much like the
rest of us. Some will be very able and some will have great difficulty with
the curriculum. Some will be outgoing and friendly and easy to get on
with and others will have difficulty in making friends. Many children with
physical impairments, in particular, are used to being with adults a good
deal and may take time to adjust to their peer group. There is also the
danger that children with physical disabilities will attract too much notice
and be given too little opportunity to become independent. Deaf children
are likely to have a more difficult time because their impairment tends to
arouse irritation rather than sympathy and because they often have problems in communicating which makes them unsatisfactory companions.
Such children may have difficulty in demonstrating their real level of
ability. Those with behavioural problems are likely to be less popular with
teachers and may not get on with other children.

Some children require concentrated help and LEAs have dealt with this in many cases by providing units within schools which allow the necessary help for some of the time but also make it possible for the children to integrate with others, perhaps joining normal classes or at least joining their peer group socially.

Children with exceptional ability have somewhat similar needs. Like other children with special needs they need to be able to live and work with their peer group in preparation for adult life, but they also need the stimulus which comes from being with a group of like ability. There is a case for gathering together a group of such children to do work which goes beyond the stage their peers are at, perhaps studying some quite different area or going more deeply into aspects of National Curriculum work.

There is a particular problem when one child is a long way ahead of his peer group. This may occur in any school. Such a child probably needs an individual programme for some of the work and an awareness on the part of the staff that such children may tend to underperform in order to stay with their friends and not be different from others. They may well be overlooked if they are well behaved, conforming and comparatively undemanding. A school needs to be on the lookout for such children.

There is a sense in which every child has special needs in that every child is different and they may need to be grouped differently from time to time in order for those needs to be met. The presence of children with special needs which are easily evident tends to make teachers more aware of the needs of individuals generally.

There is evidence from a number of sources that integration can work well. In a study by Howarth (1987) which looked at the integration of physically handicapped children into mainstream primary school classes, parents noted the development of friendships with non-handicapped children, the personal development and increased maturity and independence of their children, an increase in their self-esteem and ability to take the rough with the smooth. They were conscious that other children were learning about disabilities and developing realistic attitudes towards them. She also notes that extra teaching resources and favourable staff–pupil ratios are important and the percentage of children with disabilities in relation to the general population of the school must be well balanced.

Lyons (1986) studied the integration of deaf children into mainstream schools. She found that although there were problems the children themselves preferred being in mainstream schools to being in special schools. They felt that ordinary schools had higher status and provided more language experience. They welcomed the social interaction with hearing children and felt that they were getting a better introduction to life in a hearing world.

Hegarty *et al.* (1981) gained a general impression from their study that confidence was greater in children in mainstream schools than in those in special schools, though less than that of their non-handicapped peers. One teacher commented: 'Our experience has shown that even pupils with severe and complex needs can be educated in ordinary schools, not only with no damage to their self-esteem but with a positive enhancement of it' (p.426).

Postlethwaite and Hackney (1988) list the following prerequisites of success for integration:

- adequate preparation before the integration takes place with a good exchange of information and visits
- adequate resourcing so that the ordinary teacher does not feel overwhelmed by the new demands and the pupil is not immediately deprived of the benefits found in the special schools
- the good will of all concerned seems to be paramount.

(Postlethwaite and Hackney 1988: 79)

Jamieson *et al.* (1977), writing about the child with visual impairment, list a rather different set of factors which determine success in integration. Although this statement concerns the visually impaired, it might equally apply to almost any disability. Integration is likely to be successful if:

The child seems confident and able to cope, not to be socially isolated or left behind sighted peers in academic terms; nor should the child with visual impairment be given so much help or extra support that school life amounts to being in a special school in miniature; the host school should be willing to accept the child, prepared to seek advice and offer help if necessary, have access to specialist equipment or materials if the need arises, and its teachers should be informed of the child's condition, progress and special needs. Integration also benefits from a supportive home. Finally integration should not be prohibitive in terms of cost or volunteer time.

(Jamieson *et al.* 1977: 213, 214)

They also list the things that might make integration unsuccessful: 'inadequate monitoring of progress; insufficient support of a specialist or non-specialist nature; a lowering of academic expectations; social isolation or teasing and insufficient regard being paid to visual problems' (ibid.: 214).

Pyke (1995), writing about the blind politician David Blunkett, quotes him as saying, 'It is important for us all to think "Yes, we have someone here who's just the same as an able-bodied person but who is facing certain practical problems" ' (p.4).

The success or otherwise of integration depends to a very large extent on the attitudes of those taking part, the children with special needs, the other children in the school, the governors, parents and teachers. If those concerned believe that integration can work and are prepared to do everything possible to make it work, then it seems likely that it will be successful.

Chapter 2

The whole school approach

It is clear from the Code of Practice (DFE 1994c) that children with special needs should be the concern of everyone in the school. Both the 1993 Education Act and the Code of Practice also make it clear that the school Governing Body should be concerned to see that all teachers 'are aware of the importance of identifying, and providing for, those pupils who have special educational needs' (DFE 1994c: 6). There is also a case for ensuring that non-teaching members of the school staff are aware of the needs of many of the children with special needs and how to deal with them. School dinner helpers, for example, will need some knowledge of the particular difficulties of children with physical disabilities and behaviour problems, as will the school secretary.

The whole school approach might be described as one in which:

- all members of staff accept a commitment to work together to provide the best possible education for children with special needs including the exceptionally able;
- every teacher accepts a responsibility for assessing and providing for the learning needs of SEN children including the exceptionally able and helping them to fulfil their potential;
- all members of staff are committed to creating the fullest possible level of integration for pupils with special needs.

Jean Gross (1993) suggests that schools using a whole school approach need:

a collaborative will amongst staff, born out of collaborative school development work in special needs, that their school will be a school for all, and that the factors that make for good practice – and popularity with the school's prospective parent clientele – are the same right across the ability range.

(Gross 1993: 1)

THE EFFECTIVE SCHOOL

Schools vary not only in the extent to which they make provision for children with special needs but also in the effectiveness of the provision made. Schools which seem to do well in enabling all children to make progress appear to have some or all of the following characteristics:

- A vision of what might be that is shared by staff and governors which is used to develop goals for practice.
- A headteacher and staff who care about children as individuals and are concerned with the development of all of them whatever their background and ability.
- A headteacher and governing body who are committed to making provision for those with special needs including the exceptionally able and who seek to make as good a provision as they can for these children and do all they can to help and support the teachers concerned.
- A teaching staff in which all teachers see it as a professional challenge to provide for the learning of all the children in their care and to solve the problems that this involves. They therefore share ideas and materials and help each other with problems, are sensitive to children's needs and properly encouraging of progress. They have high expectations of children and are optimistic that all pupils can succeed.
- A teaching staff in which at least one teacher is expert in special needs and is able to act as adviser to other colleagues, offering ideas about problems and resources and keeping up-to-date with new developments and to whom teachers can turn readily for advice and guidance.
- An overall policy coordinating provision which ensures that children with special needs are identified, that their progress is monitored and recorded, that resources are available, that teachers are aware of the school programme for dealing with this area of work and that external agencies and resources are fully used, i.e., that the Code of Practice is implemented.
- A practice of assessing individual children carefully, of working diagnostically whenever possible and then matching the programme to the needs of the child.
- A substantial central collection of appropriate resources which is properly housed and maintained, is accessible and easy to use, is classified and coded appropriately and kept up-to-date.
- A recognition of the value of information technology for children with special needs and good use of what is available.
- A positive involvement of the parents of children with learning difficulties and an attempt to work with them to help their children.
- 'Effective management of support from SEN support staff, classroom

assistants, parents and volunteers ... through clear definition of roles and use of room management, one-to-one tutoring and other strategies.'
- 'A climate of warmth and support in which self-confidence and self-esteem can grow and in which all pupils feel valued and able to risk making mistakes as they learn, without fear of criticism' (National Curriculum Council 1989: 7, 8).

INFORMATION WHICH MUST BE PROVIDED

The Code of Practice lays down the information which the school must provide. This information should be available on request in a single document for distribution to parents of pupils or prospective pupils, to the local authority, the district health authority or funding authority for the area in which the school is situated and for reference at the school. The information required is as follows (summarised from DFE 1994d: Regulation 2 and Schedule 1):

1   Basic information about the school's special educational provision:
   - the objectives of the school's SEN policy;
   - the name of the school's SEN coordinator or teacher responsible for the day-to-day operation of the SEN policy;
   - the arrangements for coordinating educational provision for pupils with SEN admission arrangements;
   - any SEN specialism and any SEN units;
   - any special facilities which increase or assist access to the school by pupils with SEN.
2   Information about the school's policies for identification, assessment and provision for all pupils with SEN:
   - the allocation of resources to and among pupils with SEN;
   - identification and assessment arrangements, and review procedures;
   - arrangements for providing access for pupils with SEN to a balanced and broadly based curriculum, including the National Curriculum;
   - how children with special educational needs are integrated within the school as a whole;
   - criteria for evaluating the success of the school's SEN policy;
   - arrangements for considering complaints about special educational provision within the school.
3   Information about the school's staffing policies and partnership with bodies beyond the school:
   - the school's arrangements for SEN training;
   - use made of teachers and services from outside the school, including support services;

- arrangements for partnership with parents;
- links made with other mainstream schools and special schools, including arrangements when pupils change schools or leave school;
- links with health and social services, educational welfare services and any voluntary organisations.

The annual report for each school shall include a report containing such information as may be prescribed about the implementation of the governing body's policy for pupils with special educational needs.

(DFE 1994d: Section 161 (5))

The governing body's report must include information on:
- the success of the SEN policy
- significant changes in the policy
- any consultation with the LEA, the Funding Authority and other schools
- how resources have been allocated to and amongst children with special educational needs over the year.

(DFE 1994d: Regulation 5 and Schedule 4)

THE SCHOOL POLICY

A school special needs policy might include statements about the following:
- A working definition of special needs which covers all aspects including exceptionally able children.
  This could be the definition in the Code of Practice with the addition of exceptionally able children.
- The principles on which special needs work is based and the objectives of the special needs programme.
  This might stress the role of the class teacher and the fact that all teachers have responsibility for the learning of all children in their classes. It might also emphasise that the programme should provide access to the National Curriculum for all children.
- The name and role of the coordinator.
  This could be a brief summary of the main points of the job description of the coordinator and a statement about the time he or she will have available for helping colleagues and children.
- The overall attitudes expected towards children with special needs.
  This might emphasise the importance of teacher expectation, making differentiated provision, being supportive, setting short-term goals and targets which the child can achieve, building on interests and looking for motivation, providing appropriate teaching and encouragement both in talking with the child and in marking work. It might

also stress the importance of individual children developing positive self-esteem.

- The methods of assessing pupils to identify those with special needs including those with exceptional ability and the criteria used to make a decision about placing a child on the special needs register.

  The Code of Practice lays down a five-stage model in which the first person involved in identification of special needs is the class teacher with support from the special needs coordinator. Circular 6/94 (DFE 1994a) states that 'Having regard to the Code of Practice, the policy must explain the school's identification, assessment, monitoring and review procedures, including the stages procedures adopted by the school' (para. 43, p.15).

- The way assessment and diagnosis of problems is undertaken.

  A school needs to ensure that children with difficulties are carefully observed and studied so that programmes can be devised to meet their needs. Many teachers need help with this and a school policy which suggests ways of checking and testing details of problems would be very helpful.

- The place and method of making checks and reviewing the progress of children.

  This should be done regularly with discussion about progress between class teacher and coordinator or specialist teacher. The Code suggests that parents and, where appropriate, the child, should be involved. The policy needs to state how this will be done.

- The records to be kept on children with special needs.

  The Code of Practice requires schools not only to keep a register of children with special needs but also a record of all the steps taken to meet their needs. The records will be passed on when the child transfers to the next school and will be needed if a child is referred to the LEA with a view to statutory assessment and a possible statement.

  Such children are very vulnerable when there is a lack of continuity and there is a need for agreement about a common format within the school for keeping more detailed and continuous records about them. This is particularly important if children are withdrawn for extra help.

  The Code lays down that the special needs coordinator is responsible for seeing that records are properly kept as well as for maintaining the register. The policy should state who will have access to the records.

- The provision for access to the National Curriculum.

  The provision to be made in the classroom and the way in which work is differentiated and tasks matched to the needs of individuals.

  This might include information on the role of coordinators in the various subject areas in helping colleagues to differentiate work.

- The way parents will be informed, consulted and involved, including getting information from them about their children and dealing with parental concerns.
  This should include arrangements for seeking parental consent to approach doctors and methods of dealing with complaints from parents.
- The way the children themselves will be involved.
- Admission arrangements as they affect children with special educational needs.
  This will be particularly relevant where schools have a specialism in dealing with a particular disability. The policy should state what criteria are used.
- The material resources available on a school basis and comment on the kinds of material that are useful.
  This might include ways in which individual teachers might contribute to the school collection of materials in the process of providing for individual children in their classes. Circular 6/94 (DFE 1994a) states that 'the policy must describe the principles governing the school's allocation of resources to and amongst pupils with special educational needs' (para. 40, p.15).
- The involvement of agencies outside the school such as educational psychologists, specialist teachers, social and health service personnel.
  The policy needs to state the points of contact and arrangements for keeping and transferring information.
- The way the skills of teachers will be developed for dealing with children with special needs.
  It is not realistic to expect much to be done about this in initial training. This means that teachers must learn on the job and the school needs to organise its work so that there are opportunities for this, often arising as part of normal work but also including the use of staff development days and attendance at outside courses. Plans for in-service training should include relevant ancillary staff.
- The way that work in special needs will be evaluated.
  Circular 6/94 (DFE 1994a) regards this as a responsibility for governors and suggests that 'The school may . . . wish to indicate specific targets against which the success of particular aspects of the policy can be measured. The school will then be able to report on the success of the policy in the light of these targets in the annual report to parents' (para. 48, p.16).
- The links which exist with other schools and arrangements for transfer.
  The Code suggests that primary and secondary schools might agree a common format for records.

A school should aim to provide for children who have special needs right across the curriculum. There should also be sections about children with special needs in the policies and schemes of work for other subjects and areas of work, especially since all children are expected to have access to all aspects of the National Curriculum. Special needs teaching in the past has tended, quite properly, to give priority to work in language and mathematics but there is now a case for considering the nature of difficulties in other subjects, especially those such as music, physical education and art where the form of expression is not language. There should also be consideration of the way in which children who show outstanding ability in different aspects of curriculum should be extended.

Special needs should frequently appear in the development plan and the cost of providing the necessary service should be carefully worked out and included in the overall budget.

The staff also need to consider how they will evaluate the success of the special needs policy. The following questions might be considered:

- How many children without statements are leaving the school with inadequate skills and knowledge in the core subjects?
- To what extent are children both with and without statements achieving the targets agreed for them in the Individual Education Plans (IEPs)?
- How confident do the staff feel about identifying children with special needs including the exceptionally able?
- How confident do the staff feel about diagnosing the problems of children with special needs?
- How confident do the staff feel about teaching children with special needs, especially those with statements and including the exceptionally able?
- How satisfactory is the record-keeping and review system?
- Do children with special needs have access to the National Curriculum?
- Are the resources adequate for work with children with special needs including the exceptionally able?
- How satisfactory is the involvement of parents?
- Are the contacts with specialist services satisfactory?
- Do teachers feel that they have been given sufficient opportunity for in-service training for work with children with special needs?
- Are the relationships with the schools to which children transfer satisfactory?

THE ATTITUDES OF TEACHERS

The whole school approach to special needs implies a common vision of the way the school might provide for these children. Teachers need to share a view that they are concerned with children as individuals and that children who have special needs are a challenging problem. This is partly a matter of how competent teachers feel in dealing with learning and other problems and with able children, and this in turn reflects the way in which the school sets about making every teacher competent in these areas.

Hegarty *et al.* (1981) found that most research into integration of children with disabilities reported fairly negative initial attitudes on the part of teachers generally towards having pupils with special educational needs who had formerly been in special schools in mainstream classes. However their research revealed that 90 per cent of teachers who actually had pupils with special educational needs in their schools felt that the placements were appropriate.

They also found the following:

• Teachers tended to be over-protective and unready to treat these children like their peers.
• Most teachers were prepared to have children with special educational needs in their classes, but were not enthusiastic about it.
• Teachers did not always take teaching them seriously.
• Teachers reacted least favourably to pupils with more than one disability and to those with severe learning difficulties.
• Some teachers were not at ease with pupils with special educational needs in one-to-one and social situations.
• There was evidence that contact changed attitudes.

Successful teachers of children with learning problems somehow manage to convey to pupils their belief in them and their ability to achieve. Teacher expectation is a very important part of this work. Bennett *et al.* (1984) found that teachers generally underestimated children more often than they overestimated them, and while this was not a study of children with special needs it applies equally to them. This finding also tends to be confirmed by HMI reports. If it is easy to underestimate a child of average ability it is also easy to underestimate a child whose language is limited or a child who is deaf or is physically incapacitated. Many HMI reports also note that able children tend to underachieve.

Chaikin *et al.* (1974) found that teachers who expected a superior performance from their pupils used more positive body language. They smiled more, leaned towards the pupil, made eye contact more and nodded in response to the child to a greater extent than they did with pupils of whom they expected less.

There is a considerable danger that children and their teachers will be affected by the label 'special needs', whether these are the result of learning difficulty or exceptional ability, and will perform accordingly. Freeman (1979) makes the following point in relation to gifted children, but it has equal application for all children with special needs:

A child must be regarded primarily as a child and any special abilities then taken into consideration only as part of the whole growing person. It is not scientifically acceptable to diagnose a child as gifted and then to explain the rest of him from that vantage point; that is, assume that a child shall behave in a special way and be treated in a special way because he is labelled 'gifted'. . . . A child is a child first with special abilities or special problems second.

(Freeman 1979: 71)

This all suggests that teachers need to ask themselves questions about their expectations of the children in their classes and their reactions to them. It is all too easy to convey to children with learning problems that not much is expected of them. The work they are asked to do should be as demanding for them as is the work given to other children, while still being within their capacity. Very able children also may tend to do only as much as they think they can get away with and may wish to keep with their contemporaries. Teachers may need to do a good deal to challenge them and provide opportunities and encouragement for them to go beyond the average performance of the class.

Chazan et al. (1980) make the following points about teacher attitudes:

It is difficult for a teacher who has not had any previous contact with a particular type of handicap to know what to expect by way of general behaviour, self-determination or cognitive achievement.

Too many allowances can be made for a child as well as too few. If the teacher is unsure of how to manage the child and uncertain how far she can 'push' him, she may well react by protecting him from learning experiences rather than exposing him to them, for example, by allowing him to repeat activities without building them in to a more advanced developmental stage.

(Chazan et al. 1980: 155)

Teachers who are aware of this danger will be constantly questioning themselves about how far a child with a disability can go. Many disabled people when they are truly motivated have shown themselves able to achieve goals which others would have deemed impossible. People like the deaf musician Evelyn Glennie and the blind politician David Blunkett demonstrate what enthusiasm and determination in the face of disability can do. The National Curriculum and the need to provide an Individual Education Plan for the child should also help the teacher to avoid underestimating children with disabilities.

The integration of children from special schools, whether on a part- or full-time basis needs a good deal of in-service education for the receiving teachers, particularly if the children have severe learning difficulties. Many people, including teachers, tend to fear those who look different from the majority and teachers need time to come to terms with their own feelings about children with severe disabilities. They need opportunities to visit the special school and talk with teachers there and see work in operation. They need to discuss what it is possible to do where a child has severe learning difficulties and how to set about it.

PUPIL AND PARENT ATTITUDES

The whole point of integrating children with special needs is that they should become normal members of the class and the school. This depends upon the relationships they manage to form with other children. Some children with special needs, particularly those who have spent a lot of time in hospitals, may be less able to relate to their peer group than other children because of their previous experience and in some cases because of their particular problems. Children with behaviour problems may find it difficult to relate to other people. Deaf children and those with communication problems may have difficulties. Children in wheelchairs may need time to demonstrate to their peers that they have similar interests. However, others with disabilities of all kinds may find no difficulty in getting on with their peer group.

Mainstream children, like teachers, may fear those who look different and this may make the integration of children with severe learning difficulties or physical disabilities especially difficult. Children will also be influenced by their parents' concerns and fears. Howarth (1987) makes the point that 'the non-handicapped can project deep feelings of inadequacy onto the handicapped and regard them as causing fear and anxiety – the roots of prejudice' (p.6).

Making a relationship is a two-way process and the other members of the class may need to make the effort to relate to children with special needs. The teacher can help this process by explaining the problems some children are coping with and their effect and asking particular children to look after others with special needs and see that they are involved. This will be particularly necessary if integration is being started for the first time and involves some children with severe learning difficulties or physical disabilities.

At the same time it will be necessary to guard against children with physical disabilities being over-protected. It may also be necessary for the teacher to talk to some children with special needs about how to get on with other children. The teacher also serves as a model for both groups of children by demonstrating respect for children with special needs and showing that all children are valued as people in their own right.

Hegarty *et al.* (1981) found that pupils generally accepted those with special educational needs, though they were often ascribed 'outgroup status' and tended to form friendships with other pupils who had special educational needs. The relationship with mainstream pupils tended to be the unequal ones of helping or caring. One pupil commented 'I was very frightened of them at first. I wondered if I should know how to talk to them' (ibid.: 468).

Parents too will have their own fears about the integration of children with special needs if this is happening for the first time. Their main fear will be that such children will take the teacher's time away from their children and they will need reassurance that the organisation of the class will be such that this will not be the case to any extent. It will be easier to reassure them if there is clearly some support for the classroom teacher, either in the form of a classroom assistant or from the coordinator spending time in classrooms working with the class teacher or withdrawing children for diagnosis or help.

Research (Hegarty *et al.* 1981; Lyons 1986; Howarth 1987) suggests that parents of children with special educational needs are generally keen for their children to be integrated. Their major reason for this is that they want their children to be educated in a context of normality. However, some parents may fear that their disabled children may fare badly in the rough and tumble of normal school life and may need reassurance.

The lesson that integration should be putting across is that all human beings are deserving of respect and have a contribution to make. The better children get to know children with disabilities the more they are likely to understand and respect them as future citizens.

PARENTAL INVOLVEMENT

The Code of Practice (DFE 1994c) makes it very clear that parents should be involved in all the decisions made about children with special needs. It points out the importance of this: 'The relationship between parents of children with special educational needs and the school which their child is attending has a crucial bearing on the child's educational progress and the effectiveness of any school-based action' (p.12). It goes on to stress the need to take parents' wishes, feelings and knowledge into account at all stages.

Parents will react differently to the initial contact with the school about their child's special needs. Some will already be aware of the problem and will be deeply concerned and anxious to cooperate with the school to do whatever seems to be necessary to help the child. For others, the information that the child is considered to have special needs may come as a shock and parents may feel that they are somehow to blame for the child's difficulties. They may even refuse to recognise that there is a problem and the school may have to work hard to demonstrate the child's needs. In this case it may be best to concentrate on what parents can do to help the child with school work.

Parents of very able children may also feel concern about whether the school is able to cope with their child and may need reassurance and involvement in planning so that they feel that everything possible is being done for their child.

In all cases the parents have a great deal of information about their child which may be useful to the teacher. Teachers should be prepared to listen to the parents and ask questions about the child's behaviour at home, his or her development from babyhood and the parents' views of the problems their child is encountering and how he or she is reacting to school.

Parents also need to be involved in the overall plans made for the child and in reviews of progress. This involvement may mean arranging meetings at times which working parents can manage and arranging for information to be translated where the parents do not speak English. Some parents with children who have literacy problems may also be illiterate themselves and it may be necessary to put communication on tape rather then in writing. In short, everything possible should be done to involve parents.

INVOLVEMENT OF CHILDREN WITH SPECIAL NEEDS

The Code of Practice suggests that

> Children have important and relevant information. Their support is crucial to the effective implementation of any Individual Education Plan. Children have a right to be heard. They should be encouraged to participate in decision-making about provision to meet their special educational needs.
>
> (DFE 1994c: 14)

The Code suggests that involving children in the planning for them is likely to make them respond more positively and enable them to take responsibility for their progress. It also suggests that such involvement will help self-esteem for children for whom this is often low. The Code also suggests that schools should 'record pupils' views in identifying their difficulties, setting goals, agreeing a development programme, monitoring and reviewing progress' (ibid.: 15). The extent of involvement will vary with the age and ability of the child but the principle is an important one.

In any group of children there are differences between individuals and a good teacher tries to organise so that provision takes account of these differences. Children come to school with different physical characteristics, different experiences, different genetic backgrounds and home environments and different abilities and interests, and most primary school teachers try to plan their work to deal with the range of abilities and interests their children represent. This becomes a problem when the needs of an individual child differ considerably from those of the majority.

Hegarty *et al.* (1981), studying the effect of integration of children with special needs, found that for most there was a considerable increase in their confidence over a period. This was less true of hearing impaired children who were more outgoing when working in a separate unit than in the main school. The level of increase of independence for most children with special needs depended on the level of supervision and staff support, on opportunities for independent action and decision-making and on motivation and whether it was the policy to encourage independence. They concluded that a school should specifically:

- have high expectations;
- give pupils responsibility;
- allow them to take risks;
- make a minimum of interventions;
- make concessions only when necessary;
- reduce excess dependence;
- ... not put up with tantrums or other age-inappropriate behaviour.

(Hegarty *et al.* 1981: 431–3)

Key factors for improving behaviour, they found, were having models of normal behaviour and firm discipline. Being surrounded by normality made a difference to behaviour patterns. The teacher needed to demand the same behaviour from children with special needs as from others.

Another important element for all children, but especially for those with special needs, is the development of a positive self-image. Freeman (1979) makes the following point:

The single and longest lasting effect that a school has on its pupils is in how it affects their self-concept. The whole system, but especially the teachers, has the potential to make or mar the way pupils think about themselves for life.

(Freeman 1979: 54)

Lowenfeld (1974) makes a rather different point. 'While in general success experiences are necessary to develop an adequate self-concept, some experiences with failure may provide the necessary ingredient for developing a realistic self-concept, which is essential for adult adjustment' (p.76).

In general teachers are concerned that children with special needs do not find themselves failing on too many occasions, but it may be helpful to remember that an occasional failure can be valuable. This is particularly true for exceptionally able children who need to understand that failure is part of learning.

The Warnock Report (DES 1978) recommended that the previous categories of disability were replaced with one category, that of special needs. This was confirmed in the 1981 Education Act. This does not mean that we need to think less about the various kinds of disability which some children experience, but that the stress is on finding the best way of educating each child taking all his or her needs into account.

Every school needs to make provision for children with special needs whether or not children who would formerly have been in special schools are part of the school population. To some extent this is a matter of the way an individual teacher works with the class. Resource-based learning may also make a considerable contribution and provision may include extra help of various kinds from other adults. Some children will have a specific learning difficulty which may be overcome with additional help; others will probably need extra help throughout school life. Very able children need work which challenges them to go beyond the normal work of their peers.

In making decisions about which children need extra help, the class in which they are placed should be kept in mind. A child of average ability might need extra help if placed in a class of very able children or conversely if placed in a class of slow learners. There is also the need to be on the look-out for children of outstanding ability who choose to function at a level which just enables them to get by.

Relationships with the peer group

It is important that children with disabilities are accepted by their peer group. Not only is this important for the mental well-being of the children concerned, but one of the purposes of integration is that children with disabilities should learn to behave in normal ways. They are more likely to do this if they are accepted as part of the class community.

Spodek *et al.* (1983) suggest that

> Teachers can explain the importance of cooperation and sharing. They can help children to understand that while individuals differ in their abilities and personalities, they still deserve the respect of all. The teacher can also look for opportunities to model appropriate social responses and to reinforce other children for their appropriate behaviour.

(Spodek *et al.* 1983: 152)

The way the teacher organises work will also help to integrate children with special needs. Seating patterns and the way children are grouped for project work may help to integrate these children. Peer tutoring in which a child with special needs is helped by another child may also help to build relationships.

Howarth (1987) stresses that it is important that the programme should be a balanced one and offer creative opportunities, providing scope for emotional as well as intellectual, social and moral development.

ISSUES FOR CONSIDERATION

* Are our governors aware of and fulfilling their responsibilities for special needs?
* Are we in agreement that we need to work together to provide for children with special educational needs? Do we see this as a professional challenge?
* Are non-teaching staff aware of children who might need their help because of their special needs?
* Does our programme for children with special needs include the exceptionally able?
* Are our children with special educational needs developing positive self-images?
* Are we giving consideration to how children with special needs have access to the National Curriculum?
* Are we making provision for children who have special needs in subjects other than language and mathematics?
* Do we demand enough from children with special needs or are we over-protective?
* Are we allocating adequate material resources for children with special needs?
* Are we doing enough to involve parents of children with special needs?
* How are we making available the information required by the Code of Practice?
* Are the children with special needs integrating with other children?

Chapter 3

Identifying and assessing children with special needs

Children with special needs, including the exceptionally able, need to be identified as early as possible. The Code of Practice (DFE 1994c) suggests a five-stage pattern:

Stage 1 class or subject teachers identify or register a child's special educational needs, and, consulting the school's SEN coordinator, take initial action

Stage 2 the school's SEN coordinator takes lead responsibility for gathering information and for coordinating the child's special educational needs, working with the child's teachers

Stage 3 teachers and the SEN coordinator are supported by specialists from outside the school

Stage 4 the LEA consider the need for a statutory assessment and, if appropriate, make a multi-disciplinary assessment

Stage 5 the LEA consider the need for a statement of special educational needs and, if appropriate, make a statement and arrange, monitor and review provision.

(DFE 1994c: 3)

Children entering the school from another school will bring records with them which may help the class teacher to identify their needs. Identifying the needs of children entering school for the first time is the responsibility of the class teacher and individual patterns will emerge as the teacher works with the children.

The Code lists the tasks of the class teacher at this stage as follows. The teacher:

- identifies a child's special educational needs;
- consults the child's parents and the child;
- informs the special needs coordinator who registers the child's special educational needs;
- collects relevant information about the child, consulting the SEN coordinator;

- works closely with the child in the normal classroom context;
- monitors and reviews the child's progress.

(DFE 1994c: 22)

When teachers take on a new class, whether at nursery or reception level or at any later stage, they should have information about the children from previous teachers or parents but this takes time to digest and teachers quite rapidly begin to come to conclusions about children and how well they are likely to do. It is important to use as many different ways of assessing children as possible because it is easy to come to wrong conclusions on too limited evidence.

When a child appears to be making very little progress, it is essential to seek information about the nature of the problem and to seek it fairly systematically. This should involve:

- Studying the child as an individual, with individual home circumstances, experience, interests, personality traits, abilities and limitations and any individual learning style and preferred modes of learning. It is particularly important to discover what interests and motivates him or her.
- Discussing the child with the parents to discover whether there were any circumstances in the child's birth and early development which might explain problems occurring later. Parents can also contribute views about what interests and motivates their child and how he or she views school.
- Assessing the child's attitude to learning and to school.
- Checking to see if the child is physically sound and that his or her sight and hearing are adequate for the task in hand.
- Studying the school and classroom context to see if there are any problems arising because of situations in which the child finds him- or herself. In the case of children of exceptional ability it is a good idea to consider whether there are any circumstances in the organisation of the classroom which hold them back. For example, are all children expected to do the same work all the time? Children with emotional and behavioural problems may create disturbances because of some aspect of classroom practice. For example, they may be frustrated by the work they are asked to do or the seating arrangements of the classroom make it easy for them to disturb other people. It is a good idea to note carefully the context of any disturbances to see what caused them.
- Studying the child's strengths and actual knowledge and skill and discovering what he or she knows, understands and can do and what is not known or understood.
- Talking with the child to see how he or she views his or her progress in learning.

No one of these approaches is sufficient in isolation. All are needed. Learning problems may be mainly due to causes outside the teacher's control, but the problems must be tackled by good teaching. It should also be noted that children identified by a class teacher as having special needs may vary according to the population of the class. In a class where many children appear to have learning difficulties the teacher may choose to register only children with the most serious difficulties, whereas some of the other children, placed in a class where the general ability was higher, might well be seen as having special needs. A similar situation exists with children with exceptional ability.

Headteachers will also be aware that the identification of a child with special educational needs by a class teacher is partly the outcome of that teacher's perception and management of that child. One teacher may see a child as having special needs where another teacher may view the same child differently. This makes it important to review the names on the register of children with special needs each year as children move from one teacher to another. The views of the special needs coordinator are of particular value here in acting as a moderator for the class teachers' views. It is important that the special needs coordinator gets to know teachers and their work well.

If the school is in an area where children with physical disabilities are placed in mainstream schools the teacher will need to discover, both by talking with the parent and observing the child, what he or she can actually do and the effect of the physical disability. Postlethwaite and Hackney (1988) make the point that: 'The needs of individual pupils cannot be inferred simply from the category of their main disability' (p.3). They cite the case of two children with similar hearing problems, one of whom worked happily when provided with a hearing aid. The other had suffered a considerable loss of confidence as a result of his disability and it was this rather than his hearing problem which created a special need.

Many children with physical disabilities will be able to learn well. Howarth (1987), for example, found that 'severely handicapped pupils placed in mainstream can and do reach levels of attainment despite the restriction imposed by the handicap, which are favourably comparable with those reached by non-handicapped pupils' (p.164). It is important that teachers are open-minded about the potential of physically handicapped children.

OBSERVATION

The teacher's observation of children is the major way in which children are initially identified as having difficulties or showing themselves to have exceptional abilities. Check-lists and testing are adjuncts to observation, helping teachers to clarify their ideas about the problems or abilities particular children appear to have. Appendix 1 gives check-lists for some aspects of reading which the class teacher can use to assess what a child can do in terms of phonics.

With very young children entering school or nursery school for the first time, the teacher's initial observation will be of how children settle down, their conversation, their interaction with the teacher and with other children, their reaction to what they are asked to do, what they do in playing, how they respond to such things as stories and so on. At a later stage there may be more obvious signs of difficulty or exceptional ability in managing school work of various kinds. Some children will be extremely slow in learning to read and write and in number work and others exceptionally able. The teacher will gradually identify children who appear to have special needs of various kinds. It is in this context that check-lists may be useful.

One of the reasons for moving away from the classification of disabilities used in the past was that it is not always possible to classify impairments under one heading. A child with a physical impairment may also have speech problems. Emotional and behavioural problems may lead to learning difficulties. Many children also experience combinations of disabilities. A deaf child will almost certainly have language difficulties and since we use language for a good deal of our thinking, such children may also have cognitive difficulties. A child who is a slow learner may also have difficulties in coordination and movement and in language development. A child with language difficulties may find it difficult to relate to people, and so on. At the same time teachers need to guard against the assumption that one disability automatically leads to another. A child may be severely physically disabled but highly intelligent.

Each child presents a unique collection of problems and it is dangerous to generalise and teachers should remain open-minded about possibilities. Teacher expectation is an important factor in determining children's performance and this is equally true for those with and without disabilities.

It is, nevertheless, helpful to consider the characteristics of children with different problems and what may be done about them. There will be children who enter school with known problems such as asthma or epilepsy or other physical defects which affect their learning in various ways. There will also be others for whom some of the causes of learning problems have still to be discovered and the class teacher can do a good deal to help to identify some of the problems and diagnose their implications for the child's learning.

A factor which is likely to be common to many children with special needs is that of poor self-esteem. Children with low self-esteem expect to fail and may feel that it is no use trying. Low self-esteem leads to poor motivation. A major task for teachers is to raise the level of children's self-esteem by ensuring that they meet some success and receive praise for it.

Children with mild or moderate learning problems

Children with mild or moderate learning problems will need extra help in grasping what other children grasp easily. They will probably produce work which is less in quality and quantity than their peers. They may contribute little to class discussion and make slow progress in all areas of curriculum. The teacher needs to observe those things which are strengths where the child works with interest and enthusiasm and is able to cope with what is on offer and analyse the areas of weakness, observing and recording errors in reading, writing and mathematics, possibly using check-lists to check what the child actually knows and can do.

Children with dyslexia or specific learning difficulty

Children with specific learning difficulties may make normal or good contributions to discussion and normal or good progress in some areas of curriculum. They may have specific difficulty in reading and writing with bizarre spelling and/or specific difficulty in mathematics. Tansley and Panckhurst (1981) list among possible characteristics of dyslexia, poor auditory discrimination of vowels, inadequate phoneme–grapheme sequencing memory for matching the written or printed sound to the spoken sound, poor sound blending and mirror imaging and poor writing of letters.

Whereas slow learners are likely to need help throughout their school lives, the children who have specific difficulties may overcome them or, in the case of those whose problem is more deep-seated, may have to find ways round the problem they have, such as using word-processing so that a spell-checker can be used (although this will not deal with words which are very different from the correct version), taping some work and so on.

Less work has been done about specific difficulties in mathematics than in reading and writing. The teacher's main task here is to understand the way in which the child's mind is working to produce the wrong answers and to help him or her to acquire different patterns. It is also important to see that mathematical work is placed in real life contexts wherever possible.

Physical disabilities

Children with physical disabilities represent a normal range of academic ability. Some may have learning problems and some may have physical problems which make certain aspects of their work difficult. They may find writing tiring, for example, and may have problems in using tools in technology. The teacher needs to be observant to identify the specific problems of individuals.

Teachers should also look out for children who are clumsy. Such children may have difficulties in physical education and may be somewhat accident-prone in the classroom. They may also have difficulty with anything requiring fine coordination and may have very poor handwriting. The teacher needs to observe how the child moves and uses the hands and whether he or she is right- or left-handed. A left-handed child who is clumsy may need tools, such as scissors, developed for left-handed people.

There may also be children with particular health problems, such as heart disease, epilepsy, asthma, cystic fibrosis, leukaemia, diabetes and others. In these cases it is important to link with parents to find out what the child can reasonably do and what to do in the case of an emergency. The school doctor also ought to talk to class teachers about the treatment of these children so that they are aware of the nature of these problems.

Hearing problems

Young children may not know that they have problems in hearing and will assume that what they hear is what everyone hears. Some children will come to school with hearing problems already identified and the teacher's task in these cases is to see that they use their hearing aids and to be aware in teaching of the needs of these children. Children with a serious degree of deafness have the problem that they have not learned language in the way that most children do and this may limit their thinking powers because much of our thinking is in words. Assessment should include information about the particular areas of language difficulty, including the errors the child makes in speech and writing.

Others may have less serious hearing problems which have not been identified. Teachers should look for the following to identify the child who has undiagnosed hearing problems. He or she may:

- hold the head at an unusual angle in order to hear;
- have difficulty in following instructions;
- frequently appear to check with another child about what the teacher has said;
- have speech abnormalities;
- show a lack of attention in discussion;
- have difficulty in differentiating similar sounds;
- have difficulties in spelling;

- have poor auditory memory;
- have difficulties in reading;
- have frequent ear infections.

Teachers can check on hearing by standing behind a child and asking him or her to repeat what is said. There may also be clues in the kind of spelling errors the child makes. For example, he or she may miss part of a word – 'pich' for 'picture', 'geen' for 'green' – or make errors in the vowels used – 'hell' for 'hill' or 'lun' for 'learn'. There may also be sequencing mistakes in spelling and in pronunciation.

Visual problems

Children with visual problems may already have their problems identified and wear glasses. However, a young child who cannot see as well as others will be unaware that what he or she sees is different from what others see and the problem may not have been identified. Teachers should look out for the following possible signs that a child has poor sight. He or she may:

- frequently rub the eyes;
- complain of aches and pains in the eyes after close work;
- complain of headaches;
- screw up the eyes to look at things;
- make frequent mistakes in copying from the board;
- ask another child or look at another child's work in order to copy from the board;
- have eyes that look swollen or red-rimmed;
- hold reading material very close or far away from the eyes;
- cover one eye when reading.

The teacher can check whether children have visual problems by asking them whether they can see details of a distant view or what is written on the board from the back of the room, or of something close at hand such as details of a picture in a book.

Teachers also need to be aware that they may have children in the class who are colour-blind. This is fairly common and most teachers are likely to meet children with this defect. A colour-blind child may have difficulty in distinguishing between red and green and possibly between blue and orange. Such children quickly learn to identify things in these colours by other clues, such as shape, and so the problem usually goes unnoticed, but it is wise to avoid colour coding which depends upon being able to distinguish by the colours most frequently confused. Children who have this problem are likely to be hesitant when placed in a position of needing to distinguish green from red.

Emotional/behavioural problems

Children with this kind of problem are unlikely to be missed, but the class teacher can help by identifying the nature of the problem. A child with a problem of this kind may:

- display excessive attention-getting behaviours;
- behave like a much younger child from time to time;
- have low tolerance of frustration;
- have temper tantrums if frustrated;
- show moodiness and apparent depression;
- show aggression to others and rudeness;
- show a high level of anxiety;
- act in a solitary and withdrawn way, making few interactions with others;
- engage in behaviours such as body rocking, thumb sucking, head banging;
- be constantly on the move and apparently unable to concentrate.

Observation and records here should include details of episodes when the child has manifested unusual or disturbed behaviour, giving information about the context of the behaviour and what appeared to set it off, how it was dealt with and with what effect.

Chazan *et al.* (1980) found in their observation of the way teachers dealt with children with special needs that there was a tendency for teachers to give too little attention to withdrawn children. Observation here needs to involve the extent to which the child initiates interaction with the teacher and other children, the range of language the child uses and, as far as possible, the child's understanding of language.

Communication problems

Some children with communication problems will be easy to identify because their difficulties are very evident. The child with hesitations and stammers, for example, will reveal him- or herself quickly, although such children may try to remain silent to avoid showing their problems. The teacher will also be aware of children for whom English is not their mother tongue and those whose English is non-standard. There may also be children who choose to remain silent, children who have difficulty with articulation and children whose speech and writing is confused. Some of the children who have speech problems may also have hearing problems and the teacher should check hearing at an early stage. Assessment here should include records of the errors a child makes, the extent of the child's vocabulary and use of sentences, problems of understanding the child's speech, the child's problems in understanding the speech of others and any particular areas of difficulty.

Exceptional ability

It is not easy to define what is meant by exceptional ability or giftedness. From the practical point of view of the teacher in the classroom any child who is well beyond the normal standard of work of the class might be described as having special needs on account of his or her ability. This view of the definition means that it depends on the make up of the class rather than any external view of giftedness. This group of children may include some who are gifted by any standard either in general intellectual terms or talented in a particular area such as music or art.

The check-list which follows was extracted from lists by various researchers and circulated to Surrey schools as part of a programme for identifying gifted children.

An exceptionally able child is likely to show some of the following characteristics:

- has at least one area of outstanding ability, whether very advanced attainment (for example, mathematics or English), very advanced ideas or interests, very advanced oral skills or very advanced drawing, painting, modelling or musical skills;
- usually learns easily and readily and is able to handle complex information;*
- has a wide range of interests and several hobbies;
- is generally superior in quantity and quality of vocabulary as compared with children of his/her own age;*
- may have ability to do effective work independently, showing perseverance and good attention;
- may show alertness or a quick response to new ideas;
- may have unusual imagination or originality;
- may be very advanced or rapid reader and may have learned to read early (often well before school age);*
- may be socially very mature;
- may have an outstanding sense of humour.

(* A child showing most of the characteristics on the check-list but not those starred is likely to be a gifted child who is underachieving educationally.)

Marjoram (1988) suggests that:

It is by *listening* to pupils talk to hear how they articulate, use their voices, develop their vocabularies and complexity of syntax, learn to marshal an argument or paint a verbal picture that we can begin to pick up useful clues. We must also *look* at behaviour, at the way tools are held and used, at the way materials and paints and words are selected and handled.

(Marjoram 1988: 38)

Some of these characteristics will be evident very early. Others will reveal themselves as the child matures and learns. There may be evidence from parents of very rapid early development and unusual interests at home. An important clue to exceptional ability is to look for anything unusual in what the child says and does. A child who makes unlikely comments or reveals unusual interests may be worth watching carefully. Discrepancies in performance are also worth investigating. Strong interest in particular areas of curriculum such as music or art may also be evidence of possible exceptional ability.

Possible areas of bias in observation

It is very easy for a teacher to be biased without realising it. A pupil from a middle-class home, who is well behaved and whose work is always very neat may be overestimated and one whose work is untidy and who comes from a working-class background may be underestimated. It is also very easy, when one meets a later child from one family to expect that he or she will share the characteristics of siblings. Teachers sometimes assume that a child from a working-class background is unlikely to be exceptionally able. They may also have expectations about children from other cultures and have higher expectations of boys rather than girls or vice versa. Most of us think that we are not prejudiced in any way, but there is a good deal of research evidence to suggest that most people have prejudices of which they are unaware. Ainscow and Tweddle (1983) suggest that 'Classroom assessment should use criterion-referenced techniques, measuring the child's performance against a set standard as a basis for planning appropriate work'(p. 51). If this is done it is a useful guard against one's own prejudices.

TESTING

Teachers may wish to use some form of testing in order to add to the information they have discovered by observation. Different tests can yield an overall picture of mental ability, show how a group or an individual compares with national norms (norm referenced tests), identify what has been mastered (criterion referenced tests) and provide teaching information. No one test can do all these things. Testing can be informal using test material devised by teachers or the kind of check-list material given in Appendix 1 which gives teaching information.

Alternatively one can use standardised tests and Appendix 2 gives a range of standardised tests available to teachers. It is important to recognise that tests, whether standardised or teacher-devised, while giving valuable information, are complementary to teacher observation and are only one more piece of the jigsaw which may not necessarily offer data which informs teaching. Children can perform differently in tests on different occasions according to their current state of health and emotional state and this should be borne in mind. It should also be remembered that many of the tests available to teachers do not discriminate well at the extremes of ability.

Pearson and Lindsay (1986) make the point that in choosing tests teachers should consider whether the information they offer will be of value for teaching the children.

DISCUSSING THE CHILD WITH PARENTS

The Code of Practice envisages that parents will be involved at the earliest possible stage. This means that the school needs to arrange a meeting with parents as soon as it has concluded that a child may have special needs or be exceptionally able. It may, of course, be that the parent has already drawn the teacher's attention to a child's special needs, but it will still be necessary to arrange a meeting to exchange information. The Code envisages that this could be a chat as the parent comes to collect the child and some information can be passed on informally in this way, but once a decision is made to place a child's name on the register of children with special needs it would be wise to have a more formal meeting since parents may have difficulty in coming to terms with their child's problems and need time to talk them through. The meeting should, if possible, involve both parents. Suggestions about this meeting are given in Chapter 9.

If parents are to contribute to the assessment of the child they need to be given some guidance as to the kind of information which is seen to be relevant as well as information they themselves think relevant. It may be useful to suggest questions which could be adapted according to the particular needs of a child, for example:

• How do you feel your child is adapting to school?
• Which activities in school does s/he seem to enjoy and which dislike?
• What activities does s/he enjoy at home?
• Does s/he show interest in books and reading?
• Does s/he show interest in stories?
• How independent do you feel your child is for his/her age?
• How confident do you feel your child is in tackling new things?

RECORDS

Class teachers will need to keep a working record which can be shared with the coordinator or with specialists, such as the speech therapist, who come into the school and withdraw children for special help. A diary may be a valuable form in which to keep this, giving information about day-to-day progress towards targets. Space can be left for the specialist to add information about what he or she has done with the child and with what results.

It is also helpful to have records which can be kept mainly by the child with checks by the teacher. These record progress towards targets, and can be taken home for parents to record progress at home. One way of doing this is to provide a loose leaf file into which the child puts work which he or she feels is good. This makes a valuable record but does mean that work needs to be done on paper rather than in notebooks.

The school Records of Achievement will also play a valuable part in giving children the opportunity to record areas in which they are succeeding. Brown (1992) suggests that Records of Achievement have the following benefits for children with special needs:

- improvement in self-concept;
- pride in recording and in celebrating personal success;
- making specific suggestions as to how the pupil may improve;
- talking points to highlight personal interests and thus encouraging communication skills;
- recognising achievements outside the core and foundation subjects of the National Curriculum;
- providing a basis for discussion at the annual review;
- reporting on subjects and profile components in the National Curriculum;
- encouraging stronger links with the pupil's home.

(Brown 1992: 49, 50)

The Code of Practice requires that the school registers children with special needs. Some LEAs suggest that this should be referred to as a Record of Support, since the word register may be disturbing to parents. The Code also requires that very careful records be kept of children identified as having special needs. Circular 9/94 (DFE 1994b) states that 'Records should be written in such a way that they can be shared with parents as necessary' (p.18). This means that the parents' permission must be asked before anything about home circumstances is recorded.

Circular 9/94 (DFE 1994b) sets out the purposes of the records the school is required to keep. The context in this case is children with emotional and behavioural difficulties, but the list of purposes is much the same for all the special needs. The list suggests that records need to be kept for the following purposes:

- to inform the school's own work with the child. A record of strategies that have worked well or less well at one stage will inform the work of the school at the next;
- to inform discussion with the child's parents and the child;
- to inform teachers at a new school, should the child move during the school-based stages;
- to provide factually-based information to any outside service that may be approached for support at Stage 3. This will enable the school to make the best possible use of advisory and support services; and
- should the efforts of the school ultimately result in insufficient progress for the child, to provide the basis for the school asking the LEA to carry out a statutory assessment. In such cases the school will need to draw upon detailed records over a period of time in order to compile their evidence in support of such a request.

(DFE 1994b: para. 50, p.18)

The Code identifies the information which should be part of the record when the class teacher puts forward the name of a child as having special needs:

- class records, including any from other schools which the child has attended in the previous year;
- National Curriculum attainments;
- standardised test results or profiles;
- Records of Achievement;
- reports on the child in the school settings;
- observations about the child's behaviour.

(DFE 1994c: para. 2:75, p.24)

We might add the following to this:

- check-lists which give specific information about what the child can and cannot do;
- collections of errors and miscue analysis which often clarify the nature of problems;
- notes of books, materials and approaches used and with what results;
- information about the child's attitudes to school and to learning;
- information about the child's confidence and self-esteem;
- information about attendance and particularly about absences;
- comment about the development of social skills.

The Code of Practice goes on to list the information which might be gathered from the parents, from the child and from other sources:

from the parent

- views on the child's health and development;
- perceptions of the child's performance, progress and behaviour at school and at home;
- factors contributing to any difficulty;
- action which the school might take.

from the child

- personal perception of any difficulties;
- how they might be addressed.

from other sources

- any information available to the school from health or social services or any other source.

(DFE 1994c: para. 2.75, p.24)

The forms illustrated in Figure 3.1 are a way of recording a first referral by a class teacher. It is suggested that this record should be accompanied by samples of work. In the case of children with learning difficulties these should include lists of typical errors and possibly performance on some of the check-lists given in Appendix 1, although the school may prefer to use check-lists at Stage 2.

This referral may lead to the decision that the child should continue to work with the class teacher and his or her work be monitored. The Code does not suggest that an Individual Education Plan be developed at this stage but the class teacher and the special needs coordinator together need to decide on how best to support the child and deal with his or her problems and how the work will be monitored. Alternatively it may be decided that the child should be moved to Stage 2 straight away or after a period of further work with the class teacher. This decision will result in the preparation of an Individual Education Plan which includes specific targets to be achieved within a given time. Future records will therefore need to record progress towards these targets.

THE INDIVIDUAL EDUCATION PLAN

The Code of Practice requires that children proceeding to Stage 2 should have an Individual Education Plan which sets out:

- nature of the child's learning difficulties
- action – the special educational provision
- staff involved, including frequency of support
- specific programmes/activities/materials/equipment
- help from parents at home

NAME OF SCHOOL
Special needs referral

Name of child ....

Date of birth.................................. Class ....

No. of days absent since the previous Sept.....................................

Academic progress
Strengths

Problems

Materials and approaches used

SATS results (where applicable)

Any other test results

Figure 3.1 Class teacher's referral form © Joan Dean 1996   *continued/...*

Behaviour and attitudes
Social skills
Parents' views
Child's views

Signed .... Date ....
Class teacher

- targets to be achieved in a given time
- any pastoral care or medical requirements
- monitoring and assessment arrangements
- review arrangements and date.

(DFE 1994c: para. 2.93, p.28)

At Stage 3 the Plan will cover the same ground but will include additionally 'external specialists involved including frequency and timing'.

The Code of Practice requires a review date to be set and suggests that the review should involve consideration of the following:

- progress made by the child;
- effectiveness of the education plan;
- contribution made by the parents at home;
- updated information and advice;
- future action.

(DFE 1994c, para. 2.96, p.28)

A suggested record for this stage is illustrated in Figure 3.2. Here again it will be important to include samples of work and performance in relation to the Individual Education Plan. This record will serve Stage 2 and Stage 3.

The school needs to consider the criteria for placing a child on the special needs register and for moving a child from Stage 1 to Stage 2, and from Stage 2 to Stage 3. The Code of Practice provides criteria for making a decision about moving a child to Stage 4 and these are given below.

If the school feels that there is a case for moving to Stage 4 and asking the LEA to make a statutory assessment the Code states that LEAs should be alert to evidence that the child's learning difficulties are particularly complex or intractable, and to significant differences between:

- a child's attainment in assessments and tests in core subjects of the National Curriculum and the attainment of the majority of children of his or her age
- a child's attainments in assessment and tests in core subjects of the National Curriculum and the performance expected of the child as indicated by a consensus among those who have taught and observed the child, including his or her parents, and supported by such standardised tests as can reliably be administered
- a child's attainment within one of the core subjects of the National Curriculum or between one core subject and another.

(DFE 1994c: para. 3.51, p.53)

NAME OF SCHOOL
Individual Education Plan

Name of child ....

Date of birth................................. Class ....

Health information

Education information to date

Current strengths

Current problems

Figure 3.2 Individual education plan © Joan Dean 1996   *continued/...*

Outline plan

Staff involved (including specialists at Stage 3)

Specific programmes/activities/materials/equipment

Targets to be achieved	Date for achievement

continued/...

Help by parents at home

Any pastoral care or medical requirements

Arrangements for monitoring and assessment

Review date...

Date discussed with parent(s)...

Date discussed with child...

Signatures

Class teacher...

Parent ....

Specialist (Stage 3 only) ....

The following might also be added:

The child:
- is having difficulty with the normal work of the class;
- is creating problems which are disrupting the normal work of the class;
- is not achieving the targets set by the teacher or by the Individual Education Plan;
- is achieving the targets but these are far below the standard of the normal work of the class.

The Code of Practice states that the LEA will seek information about non-academic factors as follows:

- problems with the child's health which may have led to recurrent or significant absences from or difficulties in concentrating or participating in the full range of curriculum activity while at school;
- sensory impairment e.g. hearing loss or visual problems;
- speech or language difficulties;
- poor school attendance;
- problems in the child's home circumstances;
- any emotional or behavioural difficulties.

(DFE 1994c: para. 3.52, p.53)

The Code states that the school is required to submit the following material:

- information, including:
  - the recorded views of parents and, where appropriate, children on the earlier stages of assessment and any action and support to date
  - evidence of health checks, for example relevant information on medical advice to the school
  - when appropriate, evidence relating to social services involvement
- written individual education plans at stages 2 and 3 indicating the approaches adopted, the monitoring arrangements followed and the educational outcomes
- reviews of each individual education plan indicating decisions made as a result
- evidence of the involvement and views of professionals with relevant specialist knowledge and expertise outside the normal competence of the school.

(DFE 1994c: para 3.8, p.39)

There will be some children whose disabilities are such that it will be inappropriate to work through the stages. In such cases the Code states that

> where there is agreement between the school, the child's parents and any relevant consultant or adviser about the child's need for further multi-disciplinary assessment or there is concern that any delay might further damage the child's development, the child may be referred immediately to the LEA for consideration for statutory assessment.
>
> (DFE 1994c: para. 3.25, p.44)

At Stage 4 parents may be supported by a Named Person who is independent of the LEA. They should also receive advice and help from a Named Education Officer within the LEA. The Named Person may be appointed at the start of the assessment process and work with the parents, offering them independent advice. He or she might be a member of a voluntary organisation or member of a parents' partnership scheme. The Code suggests that the Named Person can 'attend meetings, help parents express their views effectively, and thereby encourage parental participation at all stages' (ibid.: 41). He or she may also help parents with preparing their advice and may help the child concerned to articulate his or her views.

REVIEWS AND CASE CONFERENCES

Children with statements must have their work reviewed annually (see Figure 3.3) and there is a strong case for doing this for all the children who are registered as having special needs. For children with statements the meeting is initiated by the LEA and must include a representative of the LEA, the child's parents, a relevant teacher and the school's SEN coordinator or anyone else whom the headteacher feels has a responsibility for the child. The parents may also bring their Named Person or other friend or relative to support them. The child him- or herself may also be involved.

The headteacher is required to submit a review report by a specified date. The Code of Practice (DFE 1994c) states that 'the headteacher must seek written evidence from the parents, any people specified by the LEA, and from anyone else the headteacher considers appropriate' (p.108). The headteacher is also required to convene a prior meeting to assist in the preparation of the report. This will involve the parents and relevant staff, anyone specified by the LEA and anyone else whom the headteacher feels would be appropriate. Where the parent does not speak English, there will also be a need for an interpreter.

NAME OF SCHOOL
Special needs review

Name of child ....

Date of birth................................. Class ....

No. of days absent since the previous Sept...................................

Progress towards targets

Materials and approaches used

SATS results (where applicable)

Any other test results

Figure 3.3 Review form © Joan Dean 1996

continued/...

Behaviour and attitudes

Social skills

Parents' contributions and views

Child's views

continued/...

Family background

Views of any specialist who has seen the child

Any relevant medical information

Signed.. Date.................................

Coordinator for special needs

For children who do not have statements, the review group might consist of the class teacher, the coordinator and the child's parents, with the coordinator chairing the meeting. The class teacher will need to talk with the child whose progress is to be reviewed before the meeting so that he or she has some idea of how they view the progress they have made in the past year. Older children might be involved in the meeting.

The Code of Practice sets out a plan for the conduct of the review meeting for children with statements. Most of this would be equally relevant for a review meeting for children who do not have a statement. The items which are relevant to primary schools are as follows:

- what are the parents' views of the past year's progress and their aspirations for the future?
- what are the pupil's views of the past year and his or her aspirations for the future?
- what is the school's view of the child's progress over the past year? What has been the child's progress towards the overall objectives in the statement? What success has the child achieved in meeting the targets set?
- have there been significant changes in the child's circumstances which affect his or her development and progress?
- is current provision, including the National Curriculum, or arrangements substituted for it, appropriate to the child's needs?
- what educational targets should be adopted against which the child's educational progress will be assessed during the coming year and at the next review?
- is any further action required and if so, by whom?
- does the statement remain appropriate?
- are any amendments to the statement required or should the LEA be recommended to cease to maintain it?

(DFE 1994c: para 6.22, p.112)

ISSUES FOR CONSIDERATION

- To what extent will diagnosis of the nature of problems at Stage 1 be the responsibility of the class teacher and to what extent that of the special needs coordinator?
- Who will administer and mark any tests or check-lists?
- Who will be responsible for inviting parents to a meeting when a decision is made to place a child's name on the register of those with special needs?
- Who will be present at that meeting and who will chair it?
- What should be our criteria for moving a child from Stage 1 to Stage 2, and from Stage 2 to Stage 3?

- How shall we decide about and make arrangements for the involvement of other professionals in a particular case?
- How shall we ensure that classroom teachers get feedback from other professionals who are involved with children in their classes?
- What arrangements will be needed to provide feedback to parents and other professionals?
- What ongoing records of children with special needs shall we keep?
- How shall we arrange for parents to contribute to records of children with special needs?
- What will be the involvement of the children themselves in the arrangements?
- Shall we have case meetings for children without statements? If so, how often should we hold them and who should attend them?

Chapter 4

The organisation of special needs

Each school has to work out the best way to organise special needs provision taking into account the skills of its staff and those of the special needs coordinator and any external help available.

A school which is well organised for special needs will have the following characteristics:

- the roles of coordinator and class teacher in relation to special needs will be well defined and set out in detailed job descriptions;
- the staff will work together solving problems, reflecting on their work, supporting each other and developing their work in the classroom;
- there will be clear patterns of partnership with parents of children with special needs including regular meetings and respect for the knowledge parents can offer about their children and their contribution to the Individual Education Plan.

There is a variety of possible ways of organising for special needs. In a small primary school there may be very little scope for any special organisation and the Code suggests that the headteacher may have to take on the role of coordinator. On the other hand, the number of children who have special needs may not be very many and classes may be comparatively small. The drawback may be that the school will have only limited experience of dealing with children with special needs and this is yet one more role to be assimilated in a school where there are already too few people to have experts in different aspects of curriculum. It may be that a cluster of small schools should consider appointing a coordinator to work in all of them.

The Code of Practice dictates certain aspects of the organisation. It lays down the need to have a coordinator and the role that this person should play. It also states clearly the role of the class teacher.

PATTERNS OF SCHOOL ORGANISATION

There are a number of possible ways of organising the school to deal with special needs. One of the dilemmas schools have to face is that it is difficult to avoid labelling children by making special provision for those who appear to need it. The problem about labelling is that those labelled tend to live up to the labels and others treat them somewhat differently because they are labelled. Teachers need to be very much aware of how easy it is to do this. This is less evident in classes where the teacher works flexibly and is skilled at matching work to all the children.

The following are some of the possible patterns of school organisation.

The headteacher acts as coordinator

This will be the case only where the school is a small one. The headteacher will need to allocate specific amounts of time to this work, which may not be easy, given his or her many responsibilities and the fact that the headteacher of a small school will be in charge of a class for most of the week. It may be necessary to provide part-time help to allow the headteacher to undertake the responsibilities of a coordinator.

The coordinator has a class and also works as coordinator and adviser to colleagues

This may mean that all classes are smaller, but the coordinator needs to be free for some of the time to work with other teachers and children. This organisation requires some arrangement for a part-time teacher to relieve the coordinator of his or her class for part of the week.

The coordinator does not have a class but has a regular teaching programme of withdrawing individuals and small groups according to need and also uses time advising colleagues

Circular 9/94 (DFE 1994b) makes the following points about withdrawal as it affects children with emotional or behavioural problems. Much of what is said applies more widely to other children with special educational needs:

Any withdrawal from the classroom should be contemplated only for short periods of time and where this arrangement promotes the learning of the child and that of other children in the class. Withdrawal should be used wherever possible to help the child concentrate on his or her work, which should remain under the close direction of the class teacher. The precise conditions that apply to the child's withdrawal from the classroom should be specified in the IEP and should be understood by all who teach him or her. The conditions should include the circumstances under which the child is to be withdrawn; the purpose and duration of any period of withdrawal; the arrangements for the child's immediate supervision; and the manner of the child's return to the classroom.

(DFE 1994b: para. 38, p.16)

This would seem to overlook the stress on teachers that some children create. Where a child has serious emotional and behavioural problems it may be necessary for the teacher's well-being to withdraw the child for work with someone else for part of the time in order to give the class teacher a rest and allow the rest of the class time to work peacefully. Withdrawal in this case might be used for counselling or for training in social skills if this seems to be necessary.

Withdrawal makes good use of specialist skills but it is important that there is a strong link with the class teacher over the progress of each child and some opportunity for the coordinator to observe and assess children within their normal classroom. Work done in withdrawal time should be clearly linked to work to be done in the classroom with the coordinator and class teacher cooperating and each contributing a part of the Individual Education Plan. There is also the problem of the work that children withdrawn may be missing and there may be a problem of re-entry.

The coordinator may withdraw children for teaching, counselling or extended diagnosis of problems and then support the classroom teacher in developing and teaching the Individual Education Plan.

Withdrawal for extended diagnosis has many advantages. It is the detailed analysis of problems that is most difficult to provide within the normal classroom. This pattern is also valuable in helping classroom teachers to develop their own skills and knowledge.

The coordinator works alongside classroom teachers helping children within the normal classroom

This has the advantage that the coordinator can observe children in their normal setting and help them with their normal class work, and the classroom teacher can learn from this. It can be particularly useful where a child has been withdrawn for diagnosis or to deal with a specific problem. It needs careful planning, however, because the coordinator can spend time unprofitably if the teacher is working with the whole class.

Gross (1993) suggests that the following questions are considered to arrive at ground rules for use in this situation:

• how will the class teacher make sure that the support teacher has prior information about the schemes of work or specific lesson that will be shared?

- how will the class teacher make sure that the support teacher will be in class at times when he/she can actually be useful – for example, not in formal class teaching lessons?
- when will time be found for joint planning?
- what expectations hold in the classroom in relation to pupil noise, movement, access to resources?
- who will be responsible for discipline in the room when both teachers are present?
- when and how will the support given be evaluated?

(Gross 1993: 83)

Some of these questions also apply when a particular child is allocated an ancillary helper. In this context the school will need to decide whether the person concerned will help other children who need help as well as the child in question. This helps to make him or her less conspicuous and is more useful generally.

Where a coordinator works in the role of support teacher or where the class teacher has the benefit of another teacher working in a support role for some of the time the support teacher may undertake some of the following activities:

- Helping an individual child or a group work through a programme which has been pre-planned.
- Checking that a child is achieving the targets in such a programme.
- Helping an individual or a group with the work that is currently in hand in the class, perhaps helping them to prepare a contribution for presentation to the class.
- Developing ways of helping children whose writing and reading skills are poor to produce work at their intellectual level. For example, arranging for them to tape-record a contribution, acting as scribe for a child, suggesting ways of recording which involve drawings and diagrams rather than writing.
- Making an assessment of a child by talking to him or her.
- Taking over the class so that the class teacher can deal with individuals.
- Observing how children operate and feeding this information back to the class teacher.
- Helping the class teacher to provide for differentiation.
- Discussing work with very able children and encouraging them to develop work at a higher level.
- Demonstrating ways of working which provide effectively for children with special needs.

This is effective but expensive on staffing and it is not possible to provide this kind of help on a large scale. Some teachers may also find having a second adult in the room rather threatening.

**The school is setted by ability for some work and the
coordinator takes a set of children who need help or
who show exceptional ability and need extending**

This has the advantage that classroom teachers are left with more homogeneous groups. It is important that those who are in low sets do not
lose self-esteem and confidence as a result of this organisation.

Setting provides an opportunity for gathering together children who
are exceptionally able to undertake work at a more advanced level than
they are doing in class. If it is the practice of the school to withdraw
children for various purposes this becomes more acceptable.

**Coordinators of all subjects are responsible, in collaboration
with the special needs coordinator, for advising class teachers
on special needs in their subjects**

The National Curriculum is an entitlement for all children. In the past
schools have concentrated work in special needs on literacy and to some
extent mathematics. This is no longer sufficient. Children need to be
enabled to make progress in all subjects, although in the case of subjects
like history and geography the major need is for literacy skills. There
should be provision for special needs in the policy statements and
schemes of work in all subjects and all subject coordinators should
become skilled in devising ways of accessing the curriculum in their
subjects for children with special needs. This organisation will take time
to build up and the special needs coordinator will have an important
role in helping to train colleagues in this aspect of their work.

In this context the special needs coordinator will still need to coordi-
nate work in special needs, maintain records of children registered as
having special needs, diagnose and analyse the difficulties of individual
children, perhaps undertake some teaching of children whose difficulties
are substantial, work with colleagues to advise classroom teachers,
provide a source of information about developments and research in
special needs, link with support services, evaluate special needs work
and maintain an overview of what is happening.

**Classroom teachers are relieved at various points during the day
to deal with children who need extra help**

This is a possible way of working where the coordinator is in charge of
a class or is the headteacher. Extra help to relieve the class teachers will
be required from a part-time teacher or the headteacher and this may
not be a possibility in some schools. It also implies that every classroom
teacher is skilled in dealing with children with special needs. If this

pattern is adopted a positive attempt should be made to ensure that all teachers have the necessary skills and knowledge. It will still be necessary to find time for the coordinator to work with teachers.

Classes come together for various purposes, thus freeing one or more teachers to help those with special needs

One possibility is to provide a period of about twenty minutes daily in which everyone reads. This can be supervised in a large space by one teacher while others deal with children who have problems.

Another way of working is a team teaching organisation in which the majority of children in a pair of classes work in cooperative groups or at individual work supervised by one teacher while the other deals with individuals. Where a group or pair of classes is pursuing a common topic, it may be possible to give an inspirational lesson to a large group, perhaps using a film or television. This can free a teacher to work with a small group or individuals. The problem with this, however, is that the children being helped as individuals miss the group lesson.

Other teachers besides the coordinator develop expertise in particular areas and advise colleagues

The range of children's problems coming into the category of special needs is considerable and it is asking a lot of the coordinator to be expert right across the range. Some class teachers may become expert at dealing with particular problems because they have experience of children with them in their classes. Thus their knowledge will be available for everyone when similar problems are encountered. This means that there should be considerable encouragement to teachers who have a child with a particular problem in their class to learn as much as possible about the problem. For example, a teacher with a deaf child or a child with exceptional ability in his or her class should gradually discover what works for that child and, with encouragement to study the particular ability or disability, could become expert in that particular field.

Classroom teachers are supported by ancillary helpers

Where there are children with special needs who require a helper it may be possible for the helper to work with other children in the class as well. This will help to avoid the feeling that the child with special needs is in some way different and separate from the rest of the class.

It may also be possible for the school to employ helpers on a limited scale. It is important in this context to ensure that teacher and helpers are a team and that the helpers are very clear about the programme of work individuals are following and the ways in which they can contribute. Both Bennett *et al.* (1984) and Chazan *et al.* (1980) give examples from their research of situations where teachers have left ancillary staff too much to their own devices with unsatisfactory results. Lewis (1991) notes some of the possible problems when the teacher is not well organised. Conflicting information may be given to children who may play off one adult against another, and there may be uncertainty about the helper's role. It is important to stress to helpers the need for confidentiality about the work of individual children.

She suggests three roles for regular helpers:

* *individual helpers* dealing with individual children according to their identified needs;
* *activity managers* who look after the rest of the class while they are working at activities to which they have already been introduced, leaving the teacher to deal with individual children;
* *movers* who aim to maintain the flow of activity in the class by dealing with minor distractions such as a child feeling ill, pencil sharpening, etc.

She suggests that irregular helpers may be best dealing with individual children. If they have home/school books (see pp.93, 136) it is easy for a helper to pick up what the child is doing.

Hegarty *et al.* (1981) add to this list the role of care. There may be children with physical handicaps who require toileting and general physical care. Some will require help in mobility.

An ancillary helper may be appointed for a more general role or teachers may have regular help from parents or other adults. Teachers need to be very clear about how they wish helpers to work and to brief them well. Helpers may need training for some of the roles which are possible. They should be regarded as part of the team led by the class teacher. Many will have ideas to contribute once they have found their feet in the classroom and teachers need to be ready to consider these. Regular helpers may undertake some of the following roles:

* reading stories to a group of children and discussing them;
* reading with individual children (Paired Reading, see pp.57, 89–90);
* hearing children practise their reading and discussing it;
* playing reading and mathematical games with children;
* typing out stories or other work at the dictation of individual children or from tape-recordings;
* making tape recordings of reading material for children to practise reading with the tape;
* looking after resources and helping children to find the books, materials or equipment they need and start work with them;

- making resource materials;
- mounting work for display.

It may also be profitable for an exceptionally able child to have the opportunity to work with someone who is an expert in a particular field. There may be parents or other local people with expertise or students from local colleges or universities who would be prepared to spend time with such children.

School is supported by an advisory teacher who works with classroom teachers

In some authorities there are advisory teachers who work with classroom teachers for a short period of time. This can be particularly helpful as the school starts to work within the pattern laid down by the Code of Practice. It might be worth the school's while to spend money on advisory teachers if this is the only way to obtain such help. It can be a very effective form of in-service training if the class teacher is happy to work this way.

School is supported by a peripatetic teacher who works with groups of children with special educational needs

In this situation it will be very important that the peripatetic teacher works with the classroom teachers of the children concerned and that the classroom teachers do not feel that this is all the help that these children need. This is most likely to be a provision for children at Stages 3, 4 or 5.

School has a special unit for children with a particular disability

It will be important in this situation to see that integration actually occurs as far as it is possible. Children from the unit should be integrated into classes in the main school for some parts of the curriculum and there should also be social contact at lunch-time. Teachers and children from the main school should be encouraged to spend time in the unit getting to know the children and the teacher and seeing how they work. It is helpful if the unit teacher is able to do some teaching in the main school and main school teachers some teaching in the unit. The teacher in charge of the unit should also be involved in providing in-service education for his or her colleagues in relation to the particular disability or disabilities for which the unit caters.

Exceptionally able children are accelerated in their progress through the school

This is a very tempting solution to the problem of the child who is a long way ahead of his peer group. It is only a satisfactory solution, however, if the child is mature socially and physically and thus able to fit in with an older age group and if the problem of early transfer to secondary school can be negotiated.

Drop-in before and after school classes or holiday classes

This is not a solution to all the problems of special needs but may be a complementary way of dealing with older children who refer themselves to these classes. It avoids to some extent the stigma of being seen to need additional help especially if the school has other after school or holiday activities.

School has a central collection of resources which is shared by everyone

Many of the resources required for children with special needs may be useful to a teacher for a particular child and then not needed again for some time. There is much to be said for having a central collection of resources perhaps with trolleys which can be used to take a range of materials into a classroom. The resources can be coded according to the aspect of the National Curriculum they support, or for an aspect of reading or mathematics. A school may like to adopt an overall coding system so that everyone knows that material with a blue spot on it is material to teach phonic work or is concerned with an aspect of mathematics. This collection needs to be listed with information about the use of each piece of material and copies of the list should be available to all teachers so that they can seek out what they feel they need for an individual child or group of children. This is a responsibility for the special needs coordinator.

CLASSROOM ORGANISATION

The skill required to keep a whole class of children working profitably is considerable. Lewis (1991) makes the point that there is a need for a classroom climate in which 'there is an acceptance that all children (and adults) have strengths and weaknesses and individual differences are recognised, not ignored' (p.87).

Both at school and at classroom level attention should be given to getting the mixture of class, group and individual work which most nearly meets the needs of all children. The major problem for the classroom teacher is how to provide opportunities for working with individual children. It becomes easier for the individual classroom teacher if the staff work together to plan aspects of the National Curriculum and then look at what needs to be done to make each area accessible to children with special needs and also what can be done to extend and enrich the learning for those with exceptional ability. The following suggestions may be useful.

Placing emphasis on independent learning

Lacy (1991) makes the following points about this:

> If a teacher believes in encouraging independence in pupils, the classroom will be arranged to allow open access to resources. Shelves will be labelled ... to encourage pupils to fetch and return essential equipment; books will be easily available; staff will encourage pupils to think for themselves and help each other.
>
> (Lacy 1991: 90)

This form of organisation also gives children practice in reading where things are and different children can be made responsible for checking that things are returned to their appropriate places. The teacher is also helped to find time if children are in the habit of assisting each other before coming to the teacher for help.

Ainscow and Tweddle (1988) stress the value of involving children in discussion about how to set about their learning and reviewing what they have learned at the end of the day. They suggest that 'a teacher may spend some time introducing a topic and then ask pupils to work in pairs or small groups with the specific task of identifying issues for further discussion and attention' (p.21). They also suggest that 'engaging pupils in discussion and negotiation is an effective strategy for helping them to understand the nature and purpose of their work. Understanding has a positive effect upon motivation' (p.23).

The value of cooperative group work

The National Curriculum involves some cooperative group work. Dunne and Bennett (1990) stress the value of cooperative group work for children of all abilities. They found that when the groups were of mixed ability the low attainers gained from the discussion with other children and that able children provided stimulus for the group and did well. Segregated groups of high attainers did well as a group but groups of low attainers did not. They also found that teachers valued the independence that groups developed which freed the teacher to work with individuals and groups.

Ainscow and Tweddle (1988) put forward the following arguments for involving children with disabilities in group work:

- children must learn to live and work with all members of the community whatever their disadvantages;
- children who have personal disadvantages and disabilities are entitled to participate in a broad and balanced range of educational experiences;
- they should have the benefit of working and interacting with children who are perhaps more successful in learning.

(Ainscow and Tweddle 1988: 46)

Maltby (1984) writes of the social value of such group work for exceptionally able children: 'In this type of group the gifted children would no longer be competitors and possible academic threats to their peers but fellow discovers and researchers' (p.206).

The use of resource-based learning

Good resource material is an effective teacher. Computers, in particular, offer enormous possibilities for individual learning and are very attractive to children. Word processing may be easier for children who have physical difficulties in writing and spell-checkers may be useful for children with spelling difficulties. Concept keyboards with overlays made by the teacher may enable children to produce written work who would otherwise be unable to do so. The Code of Practice makes it clear that schools will need to demonstrate that they have made use of information technology in putting forward children for statutory assessment by the LEA.

The use of peer tutoring

Spodek *et al.* (1983) suggest that slow learners may benefit from peer tutoring. Where the programme of work for the slow learner has been carefully worked out so that it is very clear what he or she has to do, another child may very well be able to help. Goodlad and Hirst (1990) make the point that the tutors in peer tutoring gain as much, if not more, than the children being tutored. In particular they gain in self-esteem. It may therefore be helpful to older children with special needs to act as tutors to younger children.

Finding time to help individuals

The Code of Practice makes the point that children should be involved in their own programme of work and help to make decisions about it.

Primary classes are busy places and teachers will have only limited time to spend with children who have learning difficulties. It is therefore important that such children are encouraged to be as independent as possible. If they are involved in the planning of their own programme and in some self-recording, and if their programmes are at the right level for them this should make it possible for them to work without constant attention from the teacher.

At the same time it is important that the teacher is able to plan so that he or she can give some sustained attention to such children when they most need it. Chazan *et al.* (1980) note that teachers who enabled children with problems to succeed managed to find the time to give the individual child the attention he or she needed because they were well organised.

The well-organised teacher is usually very clear about what he or she is doing. Children are trained to follow clearly defined rules of behaviour and to work as independently as possible. The classroom is organised so that all children can find what they need and move from one piece of work to another with minimum help from the teacher. Children are encouraged to turn to each other and to resources about the room for help before making demands on the teacher. There is stimulating work done as a whole class with follow-up work differentiated according to individual need and ability. There is also cooperative work in groups and individual work which is differentiated but which has similar aims for all pupils. Changes of activity and movement about the classroom are carefully planned. Helpers in the classroom work as a team with the teacher and are clear about their responsibilities and contribution to the children's learning. Work is planned so that children spend the maximum time on task and as little time as possible is spent on administrative issues. Tizard *et al.* (1988) found that 17 per cent of time in infant classrooms was spent on non-work activities, such as tidying up, registration, going to the lavatory and so on.

Spodek *et al.* (1983) give the following list of actions for teachers who have children with disabilities in their classes. They have to:

- adapt organisation and practices;
- work with a wider range of education personnel;
- develop a different relationship with parents;
- be involved to a greater degree in team efforts;
- plan program for children more systematically and possibly more formally;
- review procedures to determine if they are equally effective for all children in their classes;
- learn more about children's normal and exceptional patterns of development;

- learn more about different ways of learning that are effective for different children;
- learn more about ways of teaching that support each form of learning.

(Spodek *et al.* 1983: 8)

The organisation of time, space and resources

Schools need to provide time for coordinators to undertake their role, but they also need to give teachers some time for the kind of observation and recording of progress which the Code envisages. The simpler the recording process the less time it will take. Children can also be involved in their own recording to some extent and this can be part of encouraging children to take responsibility for their own learning.

Gross (1993) suggests that a staff should consider together how extra time can be found, perhaps having a brainstorming session. Some possible ways of finding time for the individual teacher to deal with children with special needs were given above.

The organisation of the furniture in the classroom can also have an effect, particularly on children who are easily distracted. Recent research (by N. Hastings and J. Schwieso, reported by O'Connor 1994) suggests that children work at individual tasks more effectively when seated at tables facing the front. However, it is also important that classroom work includes cooperative tasks for groups of pupils and some paired work. Discussion is also less effective when individuals can see only the backs of speakers' heads. Ideally discussion needs to involve some arrangement such as a horseshoe. If the classroom is arranged for individual tasks, children need to become adept at changing the arrangements to suit other activities. They arrange apparatus in physical education and should be able to arrange tables and chairs equally well within the classroom.

Children who are very easily distracted or who distract others may work best if some carrels are made by placing tables against the wall and separating them by sheets of hardboard or cupboards placed at right angles to the wall. If cupboards are used, it is important to put something heavy on the bottom shelf or screw them to the floor so that they do not easily fall over and injure someone. Working in a carrel should be treated as a privilege not a punishment.

Children with special needs are more likely than other children to suffer if the environment in which they learn is unsatisfactory. Children with difficulty seeing or hearing are easily affected if light is poor or sound unsatisfactory. Children who have difficulty seeing may need to be taken round the classroom and the school so that they know where everything is and this will need repeating if changes are made.

Some children may have more difficulty concentrating than others. They may be more disorganised, more fidgety, clumsier, less able to handle tools and write than their peers. Evans and Wilson (1980) make the point that children with behaviour problems tend to need more space than other children since they may become irritated with or irritate other children in their proximity.

The use of space, equipment and materials to support work with children with special needs must naturally depend on the school organisation adopted. Where any kind of withdrawal operates, it is necessary to equip a space for work with children. This might also house a central collection of materials which teachers can borrow. If there is no withdrawal for diagnosis or help, then space is still required centrally for materials.

The ideal provision in a school where there is withdrawal for some of the time is a room which is furnished comfortably for the work likely to take place. Some children using the room may already associate the classroom with failure and it may help them to use what is offered if the room they come to looks unlike a classroom. Ideally such a room needs a range of flat topped tables and carrels, boarding for display, shelving for books and materials, power points for audio-visual materials and storage as needed. The room need not be very large but it requires careful planning. For many schools such a room is not really feasible, but wherever possible space used for withdrawal should be made as suitable as it can be for the work.

The provision of space for this kind of work is linked to the way equipment and materials might be used. Classroom teachers need to have books and materials available in their classrooms to meet common problems, but they need to be able to draw on a more extensive school collection housed centrally. It has already been suggested that every teacher should have a list of what is available centrally, arranged so that it is classified by the problems it is designed to meet. Thus a section on phonic work might be broken down into classifications like 'short vowel sounds' or 'two letter blends' and so on.

Where a school is trying to build up a stock of material quickly it is useful to collect together all the material which is in the school, list this and decide whether it should go into individual classrooms or become part of a central collection. Gaps in provision can then be identified. It can also be helpful to make duplicated sheets to do specific jobs as these can then be made up into booklets appropriate to the needs of individual children. The identification of what else is needed also provides a guide for future purchases.

It should be remembered that many children with learning difficulties require a good deal of repetition of the same material in different forms. It is therefore helpful to have a variety of kinds of material designed to teach each skill.

THE ROLE OF THE HEADTEACHER

DFE Circular 9/94 (1994b) makes the following statement about the role of the headteacher: 'The headteacher ... has a day to day responsibility to ensure that teachers plan lessons, create an effective learning environment, have the requisite classroom management skills and set appropriate work which is differentiated according to ability and aptitude' (para. 18, p.11). The headteacher also has an important organisational role in ensuring that special needs are properly catered for and in supporting and encouraging staff. The attitude of the headteacher towards children with special needs, including those with exceptional ability, is very important in influencing the way teachers and others feel about their work with these children. The headteacher also has a special role in relation to parents, and although the Code of Practice envisages that both the class teacher and the coordinator will work with parents to a considerable extent, the headteacher still has many contacts with parents which need to be shared with staff.

Another area in which the headteacher is particularly important is in ensuring that teachers are trained to deal with the special needs problems they are encountering. Gross (1993) notes the following:

> The HMI survey (1989) of pupils with special needs in ordinary schools found that two thirds of the primary schools they visited had SEN coordinators. In only half of these schools, however, had the designated teacher received any specialist training, and in most cases the coordinator was a class teacher with no extra allocation of non-contact time for the duties involved in the post.
>
> (Gross 1993: 84)

It is probable that as a result of the Code of Practice this situation has improved somewhat, but headteachers need to see that their special needs coordinators become really expert in their roles and that all class teachers become able to handle the majority of special needs cases they encounter. Teachers need to work together to ensure this, looking collectively at problems and at possible solutions and sharing ideas and resources. The headteacher is responsible for making this happen.

Teachers, especially if they are inexperienced, may also need support in dealing with parents. Headteachers may need to train teachers to cope with the initial meeting with parents at which the child's special needs are first discussed. While this may be quite straightforward there will be situations where the parents are shocked and unaccepting of what the school is saying and an inexperienced teacher will need support and the opportunity to discuss how a meeting went and how it might have been handled differently. This is discussed in more detail in Chapter 9.

The headteacher is also the link with governors and must keep them informed about work with special needs so that they can fulfil their responsibilities.

THE ROLE OF THE COORDINATOR

Recent years have seen many changes in work with children with special needs, which in many ways are summed up in the provisions of the Code of Practice. In the past the special needs teacher has been seen as someone who took the children posing problems out of their normal classes and to some extent relieved class teachers of their responsibility for them. The change to the idea of a whole school approach to special needs has changed the role of the special needs teacher to that of coordinator of special needs work. Dyson (1991) points out that this has been a somewhat disturbing change for those special needs teachers who have seen their role as working with children with special needs rather than that of supporting colleagues.

Dyson (1991) suggests that the present role of the coordinator 'is about initiating and supporting transformation in colleagues' thinking' (p.57). The transformation he speaks of is a matter of persuading colleagues to accept that they need to work to make provision for all the children in their classes. There is no mystique to teaching children with special needs. It is something that is an extension of the normal teaching process and that can be learned. Class teachers will, however, need appropriate support in learning to deal with children with considerable problems and it is the role of the coordinator to provide this support.

Bentley *et al.* (1994) suggest that the coordinator of special needs should be part of the senior management team of the school since his or her work permeates the whole of the school and involves every member of the staff.

Bines (1992) describes the present role of the special needs teacher as follows: 'The SEN teacher/coordinator is ... an *enabler* or *facilitator* whose prime task is to develop the expertise and confidence of all staff to teach children and young people with special needs' (p.61). He/she should act as an advocate for special educational needs, 'both arguing the rights of children and young people with special needs (and their parents) and also ensuring that both policy and practice reflect the implementation of those rights' (p.62).

The Code of Practice makes the following statements about the responsibilities of the coordinator at Stage 2:

The SEN coordinator is responsible for coordinating the child's special educational programme and, always working with the child's teachers:

- marshals relevant information including, as appropriate, information from sources beyond the school
- ensures that an Individual Education Plan is drawn up
- ensures that the child's parents are informed
- monitors and reviews the child's progress
- informs the headteacher.

(DFE 1994c: para. 2.66, p.22)

At Stage 3 specialists from outside the school are involved and the SEN coordinator:

- keeps the headteacher informed
- draws on the advice of outside specialists, for example educational psychologists and advisory teachers
- ensures that the child and his or her parents are consulted
- ensures that an Individual Education Plan is drawn up
- with outside specialists, monitors and reviews the child's progress.

(DFE 1994c: para. 2.67, p.22)

There are also other responsibilities for the SEN coordinator which are discussed below.

The coordinator coordinates the work of adults

This may involve:

- helping to develop the school policy for special needs work and organising aspects of its implementation;
- providing support and advice for colleagues including any necessary in-service provision;
- organising any additional help from parents or other visitors.

Where the school has the services of a peripatetic specialist teacher the coordinator needs to seek out the best way of using his or her services.

The coordinator coordinates and monitors the progress of children

This may involve:

- helping class teachers to identify those children in need of extra help and those who are exceptionally able;
- maintaining an assessment and diagnostic programme;
- keeping children with special needs under review;
- ensuring that children with special needs have access to the National Curriculum;

- advising on the provision for such children including the very able;
- maintaining the register of children with special needs and ensuring that the records on individual children are properly kept.

The coordinator coordinates the provision and use of resources

This may involve:

- setting up and maintaining the school provision of resources for children with special needs;
- organising the use of resources;
- advising on the use of particular materials and providing help with computer and other programmes;
- keeping colleagues aware of local resources;
- keeping the market in special needs resources under review so that appropriate purchases can be made.

The coordinator needs to communicate information about special needs

This may involve:

- ensuring that all staff are aware of the requirements of the Code of Practice;
- interpreting legal requirements for staff, parents and governors;
- acting as consultant on special needs to the senior management team;
- ensuring that all staff know about school policy and about the needs of individual children;
- keeping colleagues in touch with new developments and research findings;
- maintaining links with earlier and later stages of education;
- ensuring that the headteacher and governors are aware of the special needs work of the school.

The coordinator evaluates provision and organises evaluation involving other staff

This may involve:

- ensuring that class teachers identify and assess children in their classes who may have special educational needs;
- monitoring the progress of children identified as having special needs;
- leading the staff in evaluating the effectiveness of the overall organisation for special needs;
- leading the staff in evaluating the effectiveness of staff development arrangements;
- considering whether the school is meeting the aims of the policy.

The coordinator liaises with external agencies

This may involve liaising with:

- educational psychologists and advisory services;
- health and social services;
- voluntary bodies;
- other schools.

Ideally a coordinator should if possible:

- hold additional qualifications and/or have had successful experience of teaching children with special needs before being appointed;
- be the kind of person who is able to make and maintain good relationships with adults and children;
- be ready to continue learning in this field by studying children and their problems, reading and attending courses;
- be capable of stimulating the interest and sympathy of other teachers towards special needs work;
- be well organised so that he or she is able to deal with the administrative part of the role.

THE ROLE OF THE CLASS TEACHER

The Code of Practice identifies the following responsibilities for the class teacher. The class teacher:

- identifies a child's special educational needs
- consults a child's parents and the child
- informs the SEN coordinator, who registers the child's special educational needs
- collects relevant information about the child, consulting the SEN coordinator
- works closely with the child in the normal classroom context
- monitors and reviews the child's progress.

(DFE 1994c: para 2.65, pp.21, 22)

In addition the classroom teacher needs to do the following:

- know the school policy on special needs and its implications for his/her work;
- work cooperatively with the special needs coordinator and other colleagues to provide for children with special needs, including the very able;
- observe children in order not only to identify those with special needs but to start to analyse their strengths and difficulties;
- ensure that children with special needs have access to the National Curriculum;

- put Individual Education Plans into practice;
- maintain good records of the work of children with special needs and the very able;
- organise the work of the classroom so that there is appropriate differentiation of work according to children's needs;
- organise the work so that he or she has time to deal with children with special needs, including the most able;
- organise the work of any helpers in the classroom so that they work as a team with the teacher and use their time profitably;
- be open to ideas and suggestions and findings from research about ways of working in the classroom to make provision for all children.

Schools will need to consider ability to manage work in special needs in appointing class teachers and it is probably true to say that a teacher who is likely to manage work in special needs well is also likely to be a good teacher for the rest of the class. Class teachers need the ability to individualise work and the ability to break learning down into small steps until the child is able to achieve.

Dyson (1992) suggests that 'every case of "special needs" can be interpreted, not as a failure of an individual child but as a failure of the system to educate that child effectively' (p.56).

LINKS WITH OTHER SCHOOLS

It will be very important for children with special needs that the transfers from nursery to infant or first school, from infant or first school to junior or middle school and from junior or middle school to secondary school are well managed. Such children are particularly vulnerable at times of change and are likely to feel more concern than the average child about transferring to the next school.

Records on these children need to be clear and full, giving as much teaching information as possible. Schools receiving children may find it helpful to have a small sample of the child's work marked with his or her full name and age and with a note from the teacher commenting on the degree to which the sample is typical, the problems it demonstrates and what has been done about them.

It is helpful if there can be visits by special needs coordinators or special needs teachers to the school from which the children will be coming so that they can talk with the teachers who have been working with the children and find out about them at first hand. It is also reassuring to the children if the special needs teacher from the next school can talk to them about what they will find when they move up. Visits to the next school by children should include information about any special provision made for children with special needs.

Postlethwaite and Hackney (1988) suggest that the following information needs to be sent on when children transfer to the secondary school. These points would be equally relevant for children moving from first or infant school to middle or junior school:

- persistent learning difficulties, their nature and the way they have been managed at primary level
- persistent behavioural difficulties and any record of home difficulties or involvement with psychiatric, psychological or social services
- any physical handicaps, sensory handicaps or chronic mental disorders together with recommended management techniques
- a note of lengthy or persistent absences from school which may have led to gaps in learning.

(Postlethwaite and Hackney 1988: 84)

One might add to this information about any children who appear to be exceptionally able or gifted giving details of the nature of their ability or gifts.

Mainstream schools may also want to develop links with other schools in the area so that coordinators and teachers can exchange information. Circular 6/94 (DFE 1994a) suggests that schools may consider sharing expensive equipment, may want to consult other schools in the area about developing a specialism and may like to share in-service provision with other schools. This could be particularly valuable for very small schools.

Mainstream schools may also wish to draw on the expertise of teachers in special schools, especially if there are arrangements for children from the special school to spend time in the mainstream school or if there are children transferring to or from special education.

ISSUES FOR CONSIDERATION

- What is the best way of organising our work in special needs given our particular circumstances?
- What are the responsibilities of our coordinator of special needs?
- How can we ensure that our coordinator of special needs has time to undertake this work?
- Have we reference to special needs including work with the exceptionally able in our policies and schemes of work in other areas of the curriculum?
- Are coordinators in other subjects able to offer advice on how to deal with special needs, including work with the exceptionally able, in their subject areas?
- Are ancillary helpers and volunteers adequately briefed and clear about their role? Do they see themselves as part of a classroom team?

- Are we managing our resources for special needs as well as possible?
- Are we doing enough to make our children independent learners?
- Are we using time in the classroom as effectively as possible?
- How can we find enough time to help individual children in the classroom?
- Are we using space in our classrooms as effectively as possible?
- Are our arrangements satisfactory for children with special needs and exceptional ability transferring to the next school? What is our evidence for this?

Chapter 5

Children with learning difficulties

Children with many different disabilities will have learning problems which stem from their disability, but some simply have problems in learning.

In many cases children with learning difficulties have low self-esteem as a result of their problems and it is part of the task of the teacher to find ways in which they can succeed and thus think more positively about themselves and their ability. Wolfendale and Bryans (1978) note that failure is seldom reversible after the age of 8 or 9. They suggest that 'Early experience of failure on the part of the child, even minimal failure, seems to have a substantial negative effect which endures and reduces the benefits of remedial help' (p.3). At the same time it is important to help children to see that failure is part of learning.

We have seen that it is very easy for teachers to give children a label which affects the way they are treated and also affects their self-esteem. Ramasut (ed.) (1989) makes the following point about this:

> The teacher makes a tentative guess (not necessarily at a 'conscious' level) at what a particular child is likely to be as soon as they meet in class, or even before that when pupils are judged by prior reports. The possibility is that selective evidence is gathered to support the guess, from whatever source available, and filtered into a cohesive pattern to fit the teacher's already formed constructs.
>
> (Ramasut (ed.) 1989: 27)

If teachers are aware that they may do this at a less than conscious level, they are in a position to guard against it and to look at the evidence they gather about a child dispassionately.

Mittler (1990) notes that 'Problems of disadvantage are common in families of children with special needs already in ordinary schools. Low achievement and social disadvantage are clearly associated, though it is important not to assume that there is a simple relationship between them' (p.xv).

It is also important that teachers do not use social disadvantage as an excuse for demanding too little of children with special needs. Croll and Moses (1985) found that teachers tended to stereotype such children. Teachers can do little about children's backgrounds, but they can see that they learn in school.

The first task in dealing with children with learning difficulties is to observe and to question what they are able to do and what they know. This is important in working with all children but needs to be done in greater detail for those with special needs. Teachers need to make some general observations of such things as the kinds of activity in which a child works best and is most confident, his or her ability to attend to what is happening, how well he or she can concentrate, what sensory and perceptual difficulties are evident, which materials and approaches are most successful, what interests and background experiences the child has and so on. It will also be necessary to find out in some detail exactly what the child understands and knows in reading and number. Can he or she, for example, name the letters of the alphabet in order and also give their sounds? Can he or she add numbers to 10 or more? The questions will depend upon the age of the child and what it is reasonable to expect, but detailed analysis is needed if the teacher is to know where to begin. It is also helpful to collect the errors a child makes, since these give clues to the way the child's mind is working and can be useful teaching information. Checklists for reading which may be helpful in this context are given in Appendix 1.

Children with learning difficulties find it more difficult than other children to deal with tasks which are effectively abstract. Sewell (1991) gives as an example a child who had sequencing difficulties and was unable to carry out tasks which involved sequencing, but was able, nevertheless, to manage the sequencing involved in finding the computer program she needed and loading the computer. Teachers will be aware that there are many examples of this in mathematics where a child may not be able to do a calculation when it is presented as a sum but can do the same calculation when it affects what he or she is buying for personal use in a shop.

Some children with learning difficulties will need support within the classroom or coaching outside it in the work which is going on but should be able to manage to work with their peer group for most of the time. Other children whose learning difficulties are greater will probably need an individual programme to meet some of the demands of the National Curriculum throughout their school lives. Both groups are in danger of developing a poor opinion of themselves and lacking confidence if the school does not help them to build self-esteem.

Montgomery (1990) notes that children with special needs have an inability to generalise from experience. They fail to notice key features and they also need to be taught much that other children learn incidentally.

Some children have specific problems which make other learning difficult, such as a difficulty with reading or spelling. These problems may arise from a number of sources, but particularly from developmental problems or brain damage.

It may be possible for some children, using a programme like Reading Recovery (see pp.75, 87–8), to overcome their problem to the point where they can cope without help with the normal programme of work. Others may continue to have difficulty and may need special provision, such as taped versions of reading material, for much of their school lives. Such children may be of average or above average intelligence and may therefore cope well within their classes provided the teacher is prepared to allow non-print material. It can also be helpful if a parent who is a skilled typist can type at the dictation of a child whose own writing ability is limited. The finished work can then be used as reading material.

There may also be children who have missed parts of their schooling and who need opportunities to catch up. Absence at an important stage of learning may create learning problems. The child finds he or she cannot do things which others can now do and this affects self-esteem and willingness to work. He or she should be treated like the slow learner or the child with specific difficulties in that care should be taken to discover exactly what the gaps in learning are and a programme planned to fill them.

Children with many other kinds of special needs will have learning difficulties. In some cases these are compounded or caused by various forms of impairment, for example, children who are deaf or partially hearing or have other physical disabilities, or children who pose behaviour problems.

It is important for all children, but particularly those with learning problems, to have many ways of celebrating success. One school, for example, had an achievement board in each classroom on which children as well as the teacher could post notices of their own or other people's success. Many schools use assembly for this purpose. Some schools have a system whereby children who succeed at whatever level show their work to the headteacher who may use stars or something similar to record the visit. Other schools use stickers of various kinds.

Children with communication problems

There are a number of different language problems which teachers may encounter in school. They may include children who:

- Come from a different culture from the majority.

This group includes children whose mother tongue is not English. There may also be children, like those of West Indian origin, who speak a different version of English. In addition there will be children, such as gypsies, whose experience is different from that of other children and who may not understand references to common experiences. Those whose mother tongue is not English and those whose English is different from the majority need to hear the same words spoken many times in relation to different activities, for example, 'It's time to get ready for dinner' or 'It's time to change for PE.'

Ideally such children need time with trained assistants who will help them to practise the language they need to learn, and in some areas this sort of assistance is provided. Help might also be given by parents who are prepared to spend time talking with individuals or small groups of children. They will need careful briefing and perhaps some training by teachers who are skilled in dealing with this particular problem, but they could offer the kind of one-to-one practice which these children need.

Children who do not speak standard English also need something of the same treatment, particularly in the cases of phrases and sentences where their speech is non-standard. Different parts of the country have different uses of non-standard language and it may be useful to list these so that they can be discussed with children who can be encouraged to practise the standard version. Teachers need to be careful not to imply that there is something wrong with the way children speak at home, merely that this is the way we say it at school. Older children may understand the need to speak standard English because it can be explained to them that it may help them to get good jobs when they grow up. It should be noted that speaking standard English has nothing to do with speaking with a regional accent. It is concerned with grammatical forms.

- Have difficulty in articulation.

Children may have difficulty with articulation because of a physical defect, because they have difficulty in hearing or because they have been allowed to persist too long with babyish speech. Articulation difficulties lead to spelling errors, and collecting spelling errors may give clues to some of the difficulties. Young children will still be learning to say some words but if difficulties persist the child's hearing should be checked and the possibilities of speech therapy explored. Teachers can help by showing children how to make those sounds that they are finding difficult.

The sounds which are most commonly spoken wrongly are s, r, l, th and sh. Sometimes a sound is omitted and sometimes a sound is substituted such as 'yeth' for 'yes'.

- Stammer.

Spodek *et al.* (1983) describe this as a situation 'in which the normal flow and rhythm of speech is disturbed by oscillations, fixations, repetitions or prolongations of sound, syllables, words or phrases' (p.28). It is an extremely frustrating situation for children who suffer from this disability and it requires patience on the part of the teacher to wait for the child to finish what he or she has to say. It also requires the teacher to encourage other children to be patient and under-standing and to treat the child as normally as possible. Undue attention to the problem may only increase anxiety and make things more difficult. Such children need help from a speech therapist.

- Have difficulty in constructing sentences.

Some children have difficulty with the actual organisation of their language. They may also talk very fast or in a disjointed way, or they may say very little and the most useful clues to their problem may be found in their written work which may include odd sentence construction. Difficulties of this kind are likely to be found in deaf children so hearing should be checked at an early stage.

Once again it may be useful to collect errors to see if it is possible to generalise from them although this is a problem which should be referred to a speech therapist.

- Are unable to speak at all or have very little speech.

The teacher needs to know whether the child is unable to speak because of his or her disability or whether this is a case of an elective mute. If the former, the child may be helped to communicate by the use of a computer with a concept keyboard and appropriate overlays and possibly synthesised speech. If the latter, the teacher should try to find out everything he or she can about the background of the child and whether he or she speaks at home, and should note whether the child is prepared to speak in the playground. It then becomes a matter of working patiently with the child in the hope that he or she will eventually break the silence.

Children who have communication difficulties will generally need special consideration from the teacher. It is important for the teacher to be sure to have the child's attention before speaking. Instructions need to be given in short sentences which are not in any way complex and they should be supported by gesture and demonstration wherever this is appropriate. The main part of the message should be put first because the later parts may be forgotten. Understanding should be checked by asking questions. These points are also relevant when dealing with deaf children.

Dyslexia or specific learning difficulties

Among the children with learning problems there are likely to be some who are of average or above average intelligence but who have particular difficulty in learning to read and write. These children require early assessment and a particular kind of individual programme.

Critchley and Critchley (1978) describe dyslexia as follows:

> Developmental dyslexia is a learning disability which initially shows itself by difficulty in learning to read and later by erratic spelling and by lack of facility in manipulating written as opposed to spoken words. ... It is not due to intellectual inadequacy or to lack of socio-cultural opportunity, or to emotional factors, or to any known structural brain defect. It probably represents a specific maturational defect which tends to lessen as the child grows older, and is capable of considerable improvement, especially when appropriate remedial help is afforded at the earliest opportunity.
>
> (Critchley and Critchley 1978: 149)

Tansley and Panckhurst (1981) summarise research findings on re-mediation for children with this kind of reading problem. They suggest that it is valuable to link kinaesthetic, auditory and visual information, that these children have problems with transferring learning from short-term memory into their long-term memory and that they need training in attending and planning behaviours. They also need to improve their skills in visual discrimination, spatial relations, visual memory and auditory-visual discrimination.

They suggest that teachers should assess laterality, oral reading (noting ability with phonetic sounds, recognising differences, reversals, directional confusions, substitutions, additions and omissions), handwriting, dictation of numbers and estimation of distances and heights, perception and coordination, listening comprehension, visual and auditory discrimination, letter recognition, rhyming, following directions, sequencing, recognising words as wholes in isolation and in context and word attack skills (use of context, phonic analysis, structural analysis).

Farnham-Diggory (1992) suggests that such children need to acquire strategies for learning, such as how to break a task into manageable parts, how to monitor their own attention and how to distribute their study time. She then suggests that phonograms are taught in isolation. Phonograms with more than one sound (for example 'th' as in 'the' and 'th' as in 'thing') should be taught together. Four or five phonograms are taught in each lesson and extensively practised to the point when they are automatic.

After learning about fifty phonograms she suggests that children begin spelling. A word can be given and the children asked 'How many syllables?' and 'What is the first sound you say?' (not, 'What letter does it begin with?'). The child says the sound and the teacher says, 'Now write it.' Children may then be introduced to spelling rules. She also suggests that it is valuable for children with this kind of problem to learn to type in a formal way so that their fingers learn normal patterns of spelling.

This is a much more formal approach to the teaching of phonics than most primary schools would normally use, but there is a good deal of agreement among those specialising in this kind of problem that such an approach is needed. Hornsby and Shear (1975), for example, set out in detail all the spelling rules in a book developed from their work with dyslexic children.

Montgomery (1990) suggests that the spelling of such children may be aided by helping children to see the roots of words or the parts that are alike and by tapping out the syllables. She also suggests that handwriting is helped by learning a cursive style from the beginning so that there is a flow in the writing. This means that children need to be taught letter formation. Teachers who have taken this approach do not usually find that it creates any difficulty in relating handwritten letters to those children see printed in their books and it means that children who develop fluency early are not held back by the slower form of writing that print script represents.

It is also important to help children who are left-handed by ensuring that they do not sit with a right-handed child in such a way that their elbows collide when writing. Left-handed children also need to hold their paper at a slope to the right so that they do not cover what they have just written.

It is also important that these children are given opportunities to produce written work which is at their level of thinking rather than at their level of writing. This can be achieved in various ways. Heller (1994), for example, suggests that some work should be paired writing with a scribe and the use of a concept keyboard with personalised overlays of the child's own language. He also suggests that they tape work for later transcription. All of these ideas produce material which is good looking and correctly spelled, thus contributing to the child's self-esteem. They also provide material for reading. It is also probable that before long computers will be available in school which will enable children to dictate to the computer and have their work printed out.

TEACHING AND LEARNING STRATEGIES

Ainscow (1994) quotes an earlier work (Ainscow and Muncey 1989) in which the authors found that the most effective teachers

- emphasise the importance of meaning
- set tasks that are realistic and challenging
- provide a variety of learning experiences
- give pupils opportunities to choose
- have high expectations
- create a positive atmosphere
- provide a consistent approach
- recognise the efforts and achievements of their pupils
- organise resources to facilitate learning
- encourage pupils to work cooperatively
- monitor progress and provide regular feedback.

(Ainscow 1994: 24)

Children with learning difficulties need a number of different teaching approaches. They need:

- work which is broken down into small steps;
- activities which enable them to practise the learning they are acquiring to the point when it is over-learned;
- work which involves the stimulus of first-hand experience;
- some collaborative work.

All these areas of work can involve some work with information technology.

Work in small steps

Children with learning difficulties need some work that is addressed particularly to their individual difficulties and that is broken down into small steps which can be seen to be taken. It is also very important for their self-esteem that they succeed in much of the work which they do.

The Warnock Report (DES 1978) makes the following statement about the requirements of children with special needs:

It is now recognised that the tasks and skills to be learned by these children have to be analysed precisely and that the setting of small, clearly defined incremental objectives for individual children is a necessary part of programme planning.

(DES 1978: para. 11.57, p.220)

This statement was made with reference to children with severe learning difficulties, but there is now a good deal of agreement among researchers and writers on special needs that this statement is applicable to all children with special needs (for example, Ainscow and Tweddle 1983; Spodek *et al.* 1983; Lewis 1991; Farnham-Diggory 1992). Lewis suggests that this is the way to build up to the tasks in the National Curriculum.

The child will be able to:

say the names of numerals 1 to 10 correctly when they are presented to him/her

write the numbers 1 to 10 when they are dictated

count correctly different objects up to 10

match the correct number of objects for each number up to 10

break 10 objects into 2 groups and write this as a sum, for example, 6 + 4 = 10

do this for all the combinations of numbers which make 10

apply this learning to a variety of objects including money

list from memory the combinations of numbers which make 10.

Figure 5.1 Work card: numbers 1–10 © Joan Dean 1996

To achieve this small-step approach the teacher must start by defining overall targets or aims. For example, a teacher might have as a target for one child 'To teach addition of numbers one to ten.' This then needs breaking down into detailed objectives which can be seen to be achieved. The programme should begin slightly below the level the child has reached already so that the first steps can be achieved easily and he or she can then proceed to new steps. Some of the possible objectives for teaching addition of numbers one to ten are given in Figure 5.1.

The items listed in Figure 5.1 will need to be checked by the teacher but work on the various items could be done with a volunteer parent or another child. Much of the basic work in the National Curriculum will need an element of this approach.

The important thing about an objective is that it describes the child's behaviour in such a way that what is to be achieved, and in what circumstances, can be observed. Although detailed objectives are time-consuming to prepare, they becomes less so as the teacher becomes more practised at it and they help to ensure that the child actually makes progress. Teachers who have tried working in this way find that it also helps them to be clearer about what they are doing with the rest of the class. This approach has the advantage for the slow learning child that it can ensure success if the steps are well planned. This is motivating and increases the child's self-esteem. He or she can see how learning can take place and can be clear about what is required and this enables him or her to direct effort sensibly. It is important to praise the child for getting each step right.

If the child does not succeed then the steps need to be smaller still. In the example given it might be that numbers one to five should be explored before proceeding to numbers one to ten. It may be necessary to do a lot of counting into groups of different objects.

As far as it is possible the child should be involved in the target setting and should be very clear about what the target is so that he or she can see progress towards it. The targets chosen might be the outcome of discussion about what the child finds difficult and where he or she feels help is necessary. At the same time they need to be part of the programme of targets from the National Curriculum, some of which the child may be able to manage without the need to break the work down into objectives.

Targets in language work and in mathematics may also arise from collecting the child's errors. Errors in calculation usually point to lack of understanding of some aspect of mathematics and programmes will be needed to set this right. Errors in spelling arise from lack of knowledge of spelling rules in many cases. For example, a child may spell words ending in -ed without the 'e' and will need to be helped to recognise the rule that most past tenses end in -ed. Some children have difficulty in knowing which words double the letter when adding a suffix. This is because they have not understood that when the vowel in the first part of the word is short you double the letter and when it is long, usually because there is a marker or 'magic' 'e', you do not. For example, in 'matting' the 'a' is short and there are two 'ts' and in 'mating' the 'a' is long and there is only one 't'. It is necessary for children to know about long and short vowels and be able to tell the difference. This may require a programme of objectives and much practice.

Practice activities

Basic skills such as those involved in reading and mathematics should be learned so well that they are not easily forgotten. New skills need to be practised and new knowledge used in new situations. A really slow learner needs many repetitions of the same material before it becomes his or her own and the teacher needs to think of a variety of ways of practising the same learning. Much practice can arise in the context of first-hand experience and collaborative work and computer programs may also provide practice opportunities. Computers have the advantage that, as well as being very attractive to children, they are teaching skill in using information technology as well as teaching or offering practice in a particular skill.

Practice may be part of activities about the classroom like shopping. Games are very helpful and so is game-like apparatus. For example, the learning of number bonds to ten outlined in Figure 5.1 could be practised by playing Snap in pairs, with each card carrying a number under ten. Each child puts down a card and when the numbers they put down add up to ten the first child to say 'snap' gets all the cards. A game like Snakes and Ladders can be used to learn words or number facts if children have to pick up a card with a word or a number question on it and respond appropriately each time they throw the dice. They can only move if they get the answer right. Children can work in pairs to check each other's learning.

First-hand experience

Children understand the language of others, whether spoken or written, to the extent that they can bring experience to the interpretation of the words. When children start school their experience is limited and it is important that all children at the primary stage of education have many first-hand experiences, opportunities for seeing and handling things, visits of various kinds and so on, and that they talk about them. These experiences will be most effective if they are focused, with the teacher clear about what he or she hopes all the children will gain from them as well as appreciating that individual children may gain from their personal observation. All children, but particularly children with learning difficulties, need such experiences in order to develop their language, concepts and skills and the teacher will need to think clearly about the language, concepts and skills he or she expects children to acquire as a result of the experience. These will need reinforcing following the experience. The experiences chosen will reflect the requirements of the National Curriculum.

It is also important in starting new work with any group of children, but particularly when some have learning difficulties, to discover what experiences, language and skills they already have which will enable them to understand what the teacher is talking about.

Collaborative work

Children with learning difficulties have, if anything, a greater need than other children for work which is interesting and stimulating and makes them think. They also need the opportunity to work as part of a group which discusses and works together to achieve a particular task. Talking about work is an important part of learning. Ainscow (1994) makes the following points about group work:

> Most of us learn most successfully when we are engaged in activities with other people. Apart from the intellectual stimulation that this can provide, there is also the confidence that comes from having other people to provide support and help as we work. If children said to have special needs are working alone for much of their time in school, none of these benefits accrue.
>
> (Ainscow 1994: 20)

Montgomery (1990) stresses the importance of enabling all children to develop thinking skills and the ability to communicate their thoughts and suggests that this is best done by discussion about work.

> Learning experiences are best understood and internalised when the children *discuss as they experience* and put their ideas into words. The discussions do not have to be channelled through the teacher but are between children and structured by the task. The teacher listens to and draws the whole together. The children are then in a better position *to express their ideas more formally* in writing, through drama or in pictures.
>
> (Montgomery 1990: 11; emphasis in original)

Dunne and Bennett (1990) also make this point. Montgomery describes work with a group of 6 and 7 year olds where they were asked to discover who had the largest and who the smallest hands in the class. They then set up a shop to sell paper by the length, using hand measurements and staffing the shop with those with the smallest hands. Those with the largest hands then bought from the shop and found that they were being undersold. Thus the children came to realise that a standard measurement was needed.

Montgomery's point about this and similar activities is that they are activities which can involve all children whether they have learning difficulties or not and they involve discussion which is a form of learning. A great deal of work can be introduced as a problem-solving activity which teaches thinking skills as well as the particular knowledge or concepts involved in the activity. With older children, a study of the local church or some other building, for example, might be approached by suggesting that they are visiting masons from another village which wants to build a similar church. The children then have to decide what they need to find out in order to take back the right sort of information. Montgomery comments:

> In planning cognitive process curriculum activities, situations need to be set up in which *pupils are given some information* but then asked to use it in different ways, to transform it, to apply rules and criteria,

to develop new and different products and processes on the basis of their operations and activities.

(Montgomery 1990: 69; emphasis in original)

Another possible group activity is for one group to prepare material which can be used by another group. One outcome of a particular piece of project work might be to create a kit of material on that project which other children, perhaps of a younger age group, could use, possibly with help from the group which designed the work.

We noted earlier Dunne and Bennett's (1990) finding from studying the effects of children working in collaborative groups. They found that high attainers worked well whatever the group they were in but that low attainers did not do well in a low attainer group.

> This seemed to be because of a lack of understanding of the task – even combined efforts failed to sort out problems. In addition, low attaining pupils were not drawn into the task in the same way as when working with a mixed ability group.

(Dunne and Bennett 1990: 22)

They also found that in a mixed ability group the high attainers were 'able to support their low attaining classmates with inputs of knowledge, as well as suggestions and explanations' (ibid.: 23). They suggest that groups of four are probably about the best size for primary children and that it is helpful to give some training in the skills of group work, such as listening, taking turns, asking for help politely, organising the work, explaining things, putting one's point of view clearly and so on.

The teachers who worked with them in developing collaborative teaching stressed to children that they should use their group to ask for help and come to the teacher only when the problem could not be solved by the group. This gave the teacher time to use in more effective ways.

Montgomery (1990) suggests that every pupil should receive what she calls 'positive cognitive intervention' every day. By this she means that they should receive a comment about the good features of the progress they have made, 'the next step which could be undertaken, how and why the work was good and how it can be improved or developed (p.160).

Dyke (1992), discussing children's writing, stresses the importance of publication as motivation:

> All pupils need ... regular opportunities of publication. For pupils with learning difficulties it is particularly important, as they have been denied any chance to make the vital connection between the construction of their own messages and the satisfaction of another party being able to read their statement, opinion or story.

(Dyke 1992: 90)

One school dealt with this by having, for a period, a post box and allowing children to write letters to each other at intervals during the day. The children who had special needs were motivated by this to write letters. In return, they received letters which they struggled to read with the result that good progress was made.

It can also be helpful in the right circumstances for one child to teach another. It is very good for the self-esteem of a slow learner to be asked to act as teacher, and older children might, for example, write stories for younger children in the school and read the stories to them. It is valuable for all children to acquire skills of writing for a particular audience, but especially so for children with learning difficulties since there will be a strong incentive to get spelling correct, put full stops in the right place and make the work look good.

Children's response to work

A further point to consider in planning work for children with learning problems is the way in which the child learns and responds to the work. Moses (1982) found that the slow learners she observed were on task about half their time compared with other children who were on task for about 70 per cent of their time. If the teacher can increase the amount of time the child is on task the amount of learning will increase. Gross (1993) suggests that 'poor concentration may mean that the child is not able to take in instructions, or forgets what s/he is supposed to be doing, or is restless in listening situations like assembly or story time' (p.103). Putting instructions in writing on an overhead projector or tape-recorder so that the child can refer to them if he or she forgets, may help. The way instructions are given also makes a difference.

Ricks and Wing (1976) make the following suggestions about talking to children with learning difficulties. They are talking about autistic children but what they say is equally applicable to children who have serious difficulties in learning. They would be particularly relevant for children with hearing problems. Infant teachers will do these things naturally but junior teachers may need to adapt their approach for some children in their classes. They suggest that the teacher should:

- give instructions one at a time
- avoid complex grammatical constructions
- supplement what is said with concrete demonstration and gesture
- speak clearly, loudly and with a rising inflection
- repeat as often as necessary
- allow time for the message to sink in and be understood.

(Ricks and Wing 1976: 116)

The actual tasks will also make a difference. Many slow learners concentrate poorly when asked to write. While it is important that they develop writing skills, it may help to improve their concentration if they are sometimes allowed other ways of recording.

Another way of helping is to get the whole class to write down what they hope to achieve in the next hour or another suitable period and then to check at the end of the time to see how much has been achieved. Setting a timer to sound at the end of ten minutes or so and getting children to record who was on task when it sounded also increases learning time because children aim to be on task when the timer goes off.

SOME SPECIFIC APPROACHES

The Reading Recovery Programme

A programme for children who are not making good progress with reading has been developed by Marie Clay in New Zealand and tried out in various places in Britain with considerable success. Wright (1994) notes that the effect of the programme is still evident four to five years later, whereas children helped by many other programmes have lost the ground they gained as time has gone on. She found very positive views about the programme from both parents and teachers. In particular seventeen of the eighteen Surrey schools which were involved in the programme decided to continue to fund it when LEA funding ceased. As this involved an individual thirty-minute period with each child in the programme each day it can be seen that this is a considerable commitment which schools would have been unlikely to make if the programme were not effective.

The programme as it stands requires special training for the teachers concerned but there are a number of issues related to it which could be of value to all teachers dealing with children who are having difficulty in learning to read.

Clay (1972) takes the view that children who are not succeeding in reading by their sixth birthday need study and detailed teaching. This teaching should be related to the specific difficulties of the individual child with the printed and written word. The teacher should make a diagnostic survey of the performance of the child. It is desirable:

- to observe precisely what children are doing and saying
- to use tasks that are close to the learning tasks of the classroom (rather than standardised tests)
- to observe what children have been able to learn (not what they have been unable to do)

- to discover what reading behaviours they should now be taught from an analysis of performance in reading, not from pictorial or puzzle material, or from normative scores
- to shift the child's behaviour from less adequate to more adequate responding by training on reading tasks rather than training visual perception or auditory discrimination as separate activities.

(Clay 1972: 3)

She goes on the suggests the things the teacher should check. These are:

- Accuracy in book reading.
  The child is asked to read a passage of about a hundred words. The teacher notes the words read incorrectly, the nature of the errors and the extent to which the child corrects them. The child is asked to point to what he or she is reading and difficulties with direction are noted. This record is then analysed to discover what the child can do and the particular problems which need to be corrected.
- Letter identification.
  A check is made of the letters and sounds the child recognises. A check-list for this is given in Appendix 1.
- Concepts about print.
  The child is asked about concepts of printed language. For example, whether he or she knows what a word is, a letter, big and little letters, uses of punctuation and so on.
- 'Ready to read' word test.
  This is a check to see whether the child can read fifteen of the forty-five words used in a New Zealand reading scheme.
- Writing vocabulary.
  The teacher examines examples of the child's writing looking at letter formation, and words which the child can write from memory with the letters correctly sequenced.

Tansley and Panckhurst (1981) describe a typical tutoring session as including the following:

- re-reading of two or more familiar books
- letter identification (plastic letters on a magnetic board)
- writing a story
- sound analysis of words
- cut-up story to be re-arranged
- new book introduced
- new book attempted.

(Tansley and Panckhurst 1981: 255)

Involving parents in children's reading

Many schools are now involving parents in helping their children with reading and some are beginning to involve them in mathematical work. Parents are the natural teachers of their own children and have already taught them many things in an incidental way before they come to school. Parents whose children are having difficulty in learning are usually anxious about them and most welcome the opportunity to contribute something to their children's learning. Virtually all the experimental work that has been done with parents helping with children's reading shows improvement in attitudes on the part of the children and most show considerable improvement in reading skills. Topping (Topping and Wolfendale 1985) reports that the various studies in Paired Reading, for example, show gains in reading ability of the order of three times the 'normal' rates of progress for reading accuracy and five times the 'normal' rates for reading comprehension.

Paired Reading involves a child reading aloud with a partner and giving a signal when he or she feels sufficiently confident to continue reading alone. An important element in this, as in all the studies, is that parents should be trained to give praise when the child decides to read alone. Topping makes the following point about praise:

> Neither teachers nor parents tend to be very good at praising frequently spontaneously, and if left to their own devices both groups make negative corrective utterances much more frequently, so guidance and training in this can form a valuable part of a parental involvement project.
>
> (Topping and Wolfendale 1985: 24)

Involving parents in the reading programme requires time and effort, but many schools feel that the progress children make as a result is worth it. Running a training programme may involve trying to arrange for other parents to staff a crèche so that those with younger children can concentrate on the training. It may also involve preparing a booklet of information for parents, giving demonstrations of the method of hearing reading which is being proposed and then either giving parents practice at the meeting with their own children or using role play. Topping (ibid.) concluded that home visiting by teachers also made a difference to the results, but in a later article (Topping and Lindsay 1992) questions whether it is cost effective, bearing in mind that considerable time is involved.

Another approach to parental support for reading is Pause, Prompt and Praise. Topping (Topping and Wolfendale 1985) describes it like this:

> When a child is stuck on a word or makes an error parents are asked to pause to allow self-correction, and if this does not occur to make

a tripartite discrimination as to the nature of the error made. If the mistake makes no sense, the parent prompts the child with clues about the meaning of the story. If the mistake does make sense, the parent prompts with clues about the way the word looks. If the child stops and says nothing, the parent prompts by asking the child to read to the end of the sentence, or re-read from the beginning of the sentence (to search for contextual clues). If the error word is not read correctly after two prompts the parent tells the child what the word is.

(Topping and Wolfendale 1985: 166)

The parent also praises the child each time he or she manages to get the word right after a prompt.

It is also important to consider how books are to be selected for this work and the methods of communication between home and school. Most schools undertaking work with parents develop record cards which the parent signs each day as the reading is undertaken and there is space for both parents and teacher to comment. Usually the parent is asked to work with the child for not more than fifteen minutes each day.

Connor (1994) suggests that what seems to matter with Paired Reading is:

• suitable choice of material such that the child can read independently a high proportion of the words
• parental willingness to allow children time to think or self-correct, and the ability to switch smoothly back to simultaneous reading after errors in independent reading.

(Connor 1994: 116)

Schools also have to consider which children should be involved in this kind of activity. Some include all children and start very early so as to pre-empt failure. Some nursery schools and classes involve parents in reading stories to their children and discussing them. Other schools concentrate on a few children with serious problems.

In undertaking this kind of project a school needs to plan how it will be evaluated. Some projects have used a control group, but this seems unfair. If the project really benefits the children taking part, then no children should be denied the opportunity. One possibility is to make sure that there are good records of each child's normal progress against which the progress made with parents helping can be judged.

There are a number of problems which schools may encounter in trying to implement this kind of programme. There may be parents who do not read English or have literacy problems of their own. There may be others who do not want to take part. This means that the school needs to find ways of providing for these children. It may be possible to use an older child as a partner, and in this case the older child will need some training in how the scheme works. Alternatively, other adults may be willing to take part. Some governors or non-teaching staff may be willing to contribute time to children whose parents for one reason or another are not involved and there may be other people in the area who would be willing to take part. In the case of parents who do not read English there may be older children in the home who would be prepared to help.

Knapman (1985) lists a number of things which can go wrong with reading support at home:

- reading sessions occurring too late in the evening
- individual reading sessions lasting too long or being spaced too far apart
- reading work taking place in an inappropriate setting
- parents exerting too much pressure on reading
- reading work spoilt by anxiety or loss of temper
- the use of inappropriate reading material
- parents giving too much time to mistakes or difficulties and insufficient attention to praise and encouragement
- incorrect or inadequate cues given when a child becomes 'stuck'
- imprudent use of siblings, relations, friends etc for reading work.

(Knapman 1985: 75)

RECORDS

The work of children with learning difficulties requires detailed recording and it is helpful to plan so that the child can do some of the recording. This saves the teacher time and is an incentive to the child. Figure 5.2 is a suggested form of record for the maths programme discussed on p.81. It is suggested that the teacher decides on a particular type of object for counting in the first place and then gives the child other things to count. This record sheet allows children to tick the pupil box when they think they really know the item listed, perhaps getting another child to check them. The teacher can then check and date the item when he or she has time. It will be necessary for the teacher to explain and provide materials for some items, but some will be clear to the child and if he or she can do the first two or three items this is a good incentive. This sort of record also makes clear to the pupil what the target is and what he or she has to do to achieve it.

Teachers will also need to make notes about the child's approach and attitude to work and in the case of a child posing behaviour problems teachers will need to note the frequency and nature of problems and the extent to which the programme is working to make things better.

WORK RECORD FOR..			
	Pupil	Teacher	Date
I know what numbers 1–10 look like	☐	☐	▭
I can write numbers 1–10	☐	☐	▭
I can count (bricks, money, pebbles) 1–10	☐	☐	▭
I can make sets of things for all the numbers 1–10	☐	☐	▭
I can break 10 things into 2 sets and write the sum	☐	☐	▭
I can do this for all the pairs of numbers to 10	☐	☐	▭
I know all the pairs of things in the shop that cost 10p	☐	☐	▭
I can remember all the pairs of numbers that make 10	☐	☐	▭

Figure 5.2 Work record: numbers 1–10 © Joan Dean 1996

Ainscow and Tweddle (1988) stress the value of discussing and nego-tiating work with children and of getting them to discuss what they feel they have learned at the end of a session. One possibility with older children is for each child to have a notebook to record daily what has been achieved with comments about how he or she found the work and whether it was enjoyable or difficult. This can be preceded by discussion in pairs so that children have time to think out what they want to say.

These notebooks then give the teacher a good deal of information about how children are reacting to their work. If parents are involved then the notebooks could include comments by the parents on the child's progress.

MATERIALS AND EQUIPMENT

If teachers are to differentiate work according to the needs of children in the class they need to have a variety of material which teaches to the same ends in different ways. It is valuable if groups of teachers work together to provide these so that the labour is shared. Volunteer parents can also help in putting some material on tape, duplicating worksheet material, helping to make apparatus and games, laminating material, typing, perhaps at the dictation of children who find difficulty in writing but also to help teachers provide material, and in organising and labelling materials.

A child who has learning difficulties needs to use a variety of material which has the same teaching purpose so that he or she gets plenty of practice and gradually learns so well that the learning is not forgotten.

Lewis (1991) makes the following points, among others, about work-sheets for children with learning difficulties:

- use material that is within or close to the child's experience
- introduce new concepts in a familiar context or setting (if possible try out several versions of a work sheet)
- write in language which is easily understood
- leave a wide border round the edge of the work sheet
- use short sentences and simple sentence structure
- use type or print, not handwriting
- use sub-headings to structure the work sheet
- use illustrations
- highlight instructions in some way (e.g. boxed)
- use active rather than passive verbs
- use the pupils' feedback to decide whether or not the written sheets fulfil your educational aims and objectives
- supplement with a taped version of the task sheet.

(Lewis 1991: 64)

There will be other situations where learning materials which the class is using can be adapted for those with learning difficulties. They may need adapting in the following ways:

- Simplify the language so that it can be more easily understood. This may involve making sentences shorter, changing words for simpler ones and changing complex sentences for simpler ones.

- Reduce the content if it seems more than a child is likely to be able to cover.
- Add concrete examples so that the child can see what is required and link the material with the child's experience.

Initially this is a tedious task but once done it can be used as often as it is necessary and a teacher can gradually build up material related to the National Curriculum which has been suitably simplified. It is helpful if teachers work together to develop material of this kind.

Computers

Computers offer many things to children with learning difficulties. Programs which offer practice in, for example, simple arithmetic or aspects of word building and reading give children a chance to practise and get feedback without feeling that they are being judged by the teacher. The computer will allow them to go over the same ground as many times as they feel they need.

Word processing allows drafting of written work and correction of spelling with a spell-checker – although spell-checkers only work if the spelling is sufficiently near to the correct version to be recognisable. A printer also provides the chance for children to see a really good-looking version of what they have drafted.

The use of a concept keyboard with an overlay which can be prepared by the teacher also provides the opportunity for children with serious reading problems to produce good-looking written work. Here the child touches the 'concepts' he or she wishes to include in the writing and the words appear on the screen.

Problem-solving programmes, such as Granny's Garden, also encourage thinking skills.

For children with serious physical disabilities computers have many uses. Switches which can be worked by any part of the body over which the child has control enable children with little or no speech to communicate. This can be in terms of synthesised speech or writing.

Hegarty (1991) makes the following points about the use of computers with children with special needs:

> The wide range of disabilities of users makes it a clinical art to enable access; experienced professionals within a multi-disciplinary team are needed to assess the individual requirements of users and mix and match the available equipment for them. Sometimes new fixtures or devices need to be customised for individuals. Intensive teaching and encouragement may be needed for the individual to learn to access the software and to enjoy using it.
>
> (Hegarty 1991:146)

ISSUES FOR CONSIDERATION

- How can we ensure that children with special needs develop high self-esteem and do not feel themselves to be failures?
- How can we avoid stereotyping children on account of their disabilities, social or ethnic backgrounds?
- What provision do we make for children who have been absent for a considerable period?
- What do we do to celebrate success? Does every child become involved in this at some stage?
- Are we satisfied with what we are doing for children whose mother tongue is not English?
- Are we satisfied with what we are doing for other children who have communication difficulties?
- Are we satisfied with what we are doing for dyslexic children?
- Are we breaking targets into small steps for children with learning difficulties? Could we do more to help each other with this?
- Have we enough different strategies for providing practice for children with learning difficulties? Do we share ideas about this?
- Do children with special needs, including the exceptionally able, get enough opportunities for learning at first hand?
- Are we providing enough cooperative group work in our classes?
- What proportion of the time available are children with special needs on task?
- Are we involving parents in hearing their children read?
- Are we happy with the records we are keeping? Are they easy to maintain and do they give us the information we need?
- Are we making sufficient use of information technology with children with special needs and the exceptionally able?

Chapter 6

Emotional and behavioural problems

In practice problems of behaviour are bound up with learning problems. Learning involves motivation, ability to concentrate, stay on task and so on. However, children whose behaviour differs from the norm pose particular problems for schools and teachers and it is for this reason that a separate chapter is devoted to them.

There are many reasons why children become maladjusted and the more obvious ones such as defects in sight, hearing and physical development should be checked. Some may be frustrated by the inability to learn and have low self-esteem and this should be considered. Other causes, which may be to do with family background and the child's upbringing or may be genetic, are outside the control of the teacher, who needs to be sympathetic where this is appropriate but to concentrate on helping the child to learn.

Many children who manifest emotional and behavioural difficulties have problems in their home background. Montgomery (1990) summarises some of these as follows:

> Home background can be seen as providing an 'at risk' factor by failing to supply the appropriate social techniques for fitting into a larger group, or it may fail to provide basic emotional support which the child then seeks to satisfy in various and often inappropriate ways in school.
>
> Where families are under duress and there is discord and quarreling, break-up and divorce, illness and hospitalisation, children again become vulnerable and there is anxiety and stress.
>
> (Montgomery 1990: 130)

Knowledge of home background difficulties should make teachers more sympathetic to the child, but they need to avoid the assumption that every child from a broken home is going to pose problems or that every child who poses problems comes from a home where parenting is poor. The relationship such children form with their teacher may be crucial in helping them to cope with school. The relationship the teacher forms with the parents may also help them to cope and help the teacher to understand and be sympathetic to some of the family problems.

Many children with behavioural problems not only have difficulty in conforming to the behaviour expected in school but also have difficulty in getting on with their peers. There is a great deal to be said for spending time with all children discussing social skills and helping children to see their own actions from the point of view of others. Very young children see only from their own point of view but as they grow through the primary school most children gradually become able to see from other points of view. Teachers can do a great deal to help this and the school needs to consider this kind of work as part of personal and social education. It can also be part of the study of literature and drama.

DFE Circular 9/94 (1994b) makes the following points about dealing with children who pose behavioural problems:

> In the case of disruptive behaviour, teachers will wish to give the child clear guidance on what is expected of him or her; to give focused praise and encouragement for acceptable behaviour and achievement; to consider adjustments to the classroom arrangements where necessary to organise better for success (including seating arrangements, pupil groupings and the location of equipment) and to consult the child and consider how he or she can reflect on the behaviour, developments, achievements and areas for attention. Approaches that rely substantially on positive reinforcement of desirable behaviour rather than punishment of undesirable behaviour, will be more powerful in the management of behavioural difficulties.
>
> (DFE 1994c: para. 33, p.14)

Children with emotional and behavioural difficulties represent a range of problems. Some will be hyperactive and pose problems of control and some will be withdrawn and difficult to get to know. Some will be autistic. Some will be euphoric and some depressed, some noisy and some quiet. Their behaviour may include temper tantrums, mood changes, inability to tolerate frustration, difficulty in relating to other people, language problems and school phobia among other things. In many ways they pose considerable problems for the teacher and possibly for other children in the class.

In general children who pose behavioural problems need a well-structured programme with short, structured tasks which lead to quick success.

DISRUPTIVE BEHAVIOUR

Wolfendale (1992b) makes some general points about discipline in schools which are relevant in this context:

Teachers take properly and seriously their ability or inability to control (to contain or redirect) the behaviour of individuals or groups.

Simplistic sets of sanctions, invoking rules, threatening disciplinary measures, have been shown merely to contain but never to solve any of the school's problems of unrest and dissident behaviour.

(Wolfendale 1992b: 66)

This is not to suggest that rules and sanctions are unnecessary, but that by themselves they will not solve difficult behavioural problems. A school needs to have a behaviour policy which sets out what is expected and the way staff should react to bad behaviour. In particular it needs to stress that children should be praised and rewarded for good behaviour, particularly those whose behaviour needs to be modified. It is very easy for a child to get a bad name within a school and to receive continual reproofs and very little praise, even when he or she does the right thing.

Teachers also need to support each other in their difficult task of managing their classes and particularly in managing children whose behaviour really poses problems. This can be stressful and it helps if colleagues appreciate this.

Galloway and Goodwin (1985) make the point that schools exert a considerable influence on children and that whether a pupil is considered disruptive or maladjusted depends to some extent on factors within the school as well as factors within the family or the child. They found that some of the best schools in their study regarded disturbing behaviour as demonstrating a need to change approaches to learning for the child in question rather than simply attributing it to external causes.

Evans and Wilson (1980) studied teachers' views of the characteristics of the special school most likely to cope well with children with behaviour disorders. The most important of these were as follows:

- Warm, caring attitudes in adult–child relationships
- Improvement of self-image through success
- Individual counselling and discussion
- A varied and stimulating educational programme
- Continuity of adult–child relationships
- Firm, consistent discipline.

(Evans and Wilson 1980: 67)

They go on to describe the successful practitioners with disturbed children:

We observed that successful practitioners working with disturbed pupils, whether in special schools, special classes or units or ordinary schools, showed an ability to endure in work which was not only very demanding but also often disappointing. They appeared to have a reserve of emotional strength and resilience which enabled them to mobilise warm feelings of concern for children in difficulty. They were mature and did not need to respond primitively and impulsively to the often challenging, aggressive or rejecting behaviour of the children.

(Evans and Wilson 1980: 80)

They suggest that what these children most need is the kind of care which is offered in the good home, where parents are supportive of their children and on their side, wanting their children to do as well and be as happy as possible.

Successful teachers of these children get to know them well, talking with them, studying them, discussing them with their parents and with colleagues and trying to seek out some of the underlying reasons for their behaviour. They remain calm, confident and non-aggressive in the face of aggravation, remembering that example is important, both the example of the teacher and that of other pupils.

This is easy to say but very difficult to do in practice because some children will project onto the teacher their own feelings of anxiety, anger and frustration and it takes a good deal of maturity to accept that this is what is happening and to remain calm under intense provocation.

Greenhalgh (1994) also makes the point that 'A child who has been rejected, over-protected or abused may find it difficult to accept even a positive expression of worth' (p.50). This means that teachers need to be patient beyond the normal level since such children may be unrewarding for a long time. He also reminds us that 'When working with disturbing children one might find oneself feeling hurt, abused, angry, frustrated, intolerant, anxious, de-skilled and even frightened' (p.53). At the same time teachers need to remember that behaviour is a form of communication. The child who is disruptive is making a statement and teachers need to reflect on what the message might be. Children also give clues about their problems in their drawing and painting and in play and drama. The aim is to help the child to reach the stage when he or she can talk about the problem rather than acting it out.

It is also helpful to such children if the teacher uses opportunities arising in the normal work of the classroom to discuss feelings. This could arise naturally in discussion of literature or in religious education and it could be introduced in subjects like history and geography where children might be asked to consider how people felt or might feel about different events.

The Elton Report, *Discipline in Schools* (DES Welsh Office 1989), makes the following point:

We are convinced that there are skills, which all teachers need, involved in listening to young people and encouraging them to talk about their hopes and concerns before coming to a judgement about their behaviour. We consider that these basic counselling skills are particularly valuable for creating a supportive school atmosphere.

(DES Welsh Office 1989: para. 111, p.114)

Working with these children may involve some counselling and some teaching of social behaviour because sometimes children are unable to see the effects of their behaviour on others. It is also valuable to deal with some of children's misbehaviour by getting the child to think through the effect of what he or she has done and particularly, where it is relevant, the effect on other people.

Counselling involves careful listening to what the other person has to say and trying to see things from his or her point of view, while avoiding jumping to conclusions or lecturing. Greenhalgh (1994) suggests that 'Empathetic understanding involves being able to appreciate what life is like for the other person, understanding the other person's frame of reference, how the other person sees situations, relationships and the world in which s/he lives' (p.87).

Counselling also involves reflecting for the child the way his or her behaviour is affecting those around, both teachers and other children, and trying to help the child arrive at his or her own solution to the problems being discussed. It is helpful to summarise the discussion at intervals during it and at the end so that there can be a check on whether what has been said on both sides has been understood. Gross (1993) suggests asking questions like 'Tell me some of the things that make teachers pleased with you. . . . Now tell me what sort of things you do that bother them most' (p.101). She also suggests getting the child to think of ten things that make him or her angry and then to rank them in order of intensity. She suggests then teaching strategies for coping when starting to feel angry, such as muscle relaxation and deep breathing, counting to ten backwards or taking themselves to a cooling off spot on the fringe of the activity. Such children may also need to learn negotiating skills. She suggests:

Work can be done to involve pupils in considering which responses to conflict situations are likely to escalate the conflict and which diffuse it and in practising the negotiation skill of saying what you want and why, listening carefully to the other's point of view, then trying to find a compromise that meets both parties' needs.

(Gross 1993: 102)

Charlton (1992) suggests that there are three attitudes needed by people undertaking counselling. The first of these is acceptance. 'This involves acceptance of the pupil no matter how disruptive and disappointing her/his behaviour is. One way to accomplish this is to separate the child from the behaviour; the behaviour may be criticised but the child remains accepted.' The second is genuineness. 'This requires a person to be her/himself, and not to hide behind a persona. . . . People who are genuine seem to offer a sense of security and trust to those with whom they work.' The third is empathy. 'This indicates an ability to truly understand how another person feels; it is as if one person is "in tune" with another' (ibid.: 32). It may be necessary to explain this strategy to parents, emphasising that the idea is to put the child in control of his or her reactions.

Where a child poses a real problem because of his or her behaviour it is helpful if the teacher records the situations in which disturbing behaviour arises, noting the context and what appears to trigger it. If such records are kept over a period it may be possible to avoid situations which give rise to some disturbing behaviour.

It may be helpful to develop a profile of the child. Greenhalgh (1994) suggests that the following observations may be helpful:

- body language and eye contact
- anxiety level
- how the child relates to the teacher
- dependence/independence
- response to praise or failure – can the child tolerate being corrected, or bear not to know?
- response to winning or losing: can the child bear to compete or to lose?
- anger: can the child use it? Is the child afraid of it?
- does the child engage in solitary or mutual play?

(Greenhalgh 1994: 100)

It will also be helpful to know the child's home background, his or her position in the family, the parents' views on the problems and on the relationships the child has with others in the home, his or her interests and hobbies and social contacts at home and how the parents think the child sees school.

The child, too, will have views which are valuable to explore. It is helpful to know how he or she sees school and the things which are liked or disliked. Children will also have views about where they fit in at home and with peers in school, will be able to talk about how they spend time out of school and have a perception of their own needs.

Generally punishment, while it may suppress undesirable behaviour, may have side-effects. It may, however, have an effect on others. Children expect punishment for bad behaviour and may try to test a teacher to the limits.

One approach to dealing with children who are disruptive which has been successful in many cases is behaviour modification. This starts with the teacher identifying clearly the behaviour he or she wishes to change. Thus a teacher might note that a child frequently wanders about the room and disturbs other children. The teacher starts by counting the number of times this happens in the course of a morning or day. The task is then to reduce this number. The teacher discusses the problem with the child and they agree very specific goals which appear to be within the child's capacity to attain. For example, they may agree that the child will work for ten minutes by the clock without getting up or disturbing anyone else. If he or she is successful this can be recorded and the child praised or rewarded in some way and another goal set. If there is no success, a different and lesser goal can be set – perhaps working for five minutes instead of ten, until the child is able to achieve. The child is also encouraged to keep a record both of his or her successes and of the number of times he or she wanders and is encouraged to try to reduce the incidence of wandering day by day. It is important that there is initially some reward when the child succeeds in meeting the goal. This might be a chance to do some activity which he or she particularly likes or the award of a star or a token of some kind which can be exchanged for an activity when enough tokens are collected.

This is a much more specific use of goals and rewards than normal teaching and it is important that progress is clearly recorded for the child to see and that there is a reward of praise for achievement following immediately. This method can be applied very widely. It can also involve parents, particularly when the behaviour at home is similar to that at school. Parents and teachers can then combine to modify the behaviour and the parents can support the school in giving rewards. A more detailed account of behaviour modification is given by Wheldall and Merritt (1984b) who have also published in-service material on this approach (BATPACK: Wheldall and Merritt 1984a) which can be used at a whole class level as well as with individuals.

Children with behavioural problems may be both bullies and bullied. The school needs to have a policy about bullying which encourages children not only to tell teachers when they are bullied but also to report any incidents of bullying which they may see. The most effective plan for dealing with bullying appears to be to get the child who is bullied to talk to the bully in the presence of a teacher about how he or she felt.

Teachers have to deal with indiscipline as it arises and it is tempting to scold the same children over and over again. It should be remembered that children who pose behavioural problems often have a poor self-image and the teacher needs to work to change this by praising them when they do the right thing. They are also often suspicious of adults.

Nevertheless the teacher cannot allow indiscipline to continue to any extent because of the effect it has on other children. Moving towards the child, making eye contact and appearing confident are all ways of dealing with the child who is creating a disturbance. When it is necessary to make a negative comment this is best couched in terms of what the child should be doing. For example, 'Mary, have you finished your work?', rather than telling Mary to behave differently. This can have a ripple effect on the rest of the class.

It is also helpful to have a very clear set of classroom rules agreed by all the children and firmly enforced. This enables the teacher to refer to these when checking a child for misbehaviour.

Kounin (1970) studied the techniques of control used by effective teachers and noted particularly the effectiveness of the following (the labels are Kounin's):

- 'withitness' He noted that teachers were effective when they communicated to pupils their awareness of what was happening in the classroom and had an ability to target the right person for any reproof and catch deviant behaviour at an early stage before it had time to escalate.
- 'overlapping' The ability to maintain attention to one event while dealing with another. This is an essential ability for primary teachers and most are very good at it.
- 'smoothness' The ability to manage change from one activity to another.
- 'slowdown' Skill in avoiding anything which slows down the pace of the lesson and maintaining pace towards the main objectives.

A teacher may find him- or herself having to deal with an outburst from a child. It is important to appear to remain calm and to tell the child that his or her outburst will be discussed later after the class. Other children should be settled to work again and the teacher continue to deal with individuals or groups including the child who has disturbed the class. After the other children have gone the teacher then talks to the individual, sitting down with him or her and asking what caused the outburst.

At the school level, when a child is referred as having special needs on account of behaviour, the coordinator needs to check that the teacher has tried all the suggestions given above. It may be helpful to discuss behaviour with the child, asking why he or she feels compelled to behave in disruptive ways. What, in the child's view, triggers it off? What would help him or her to avoid such behaviour? It is also a good thing where behaviour involves other children to try to paint a picture of how they feel or involve them in talking with the child concerned about how they feel. It may be possible with older children to devise a contract agreeing that the child will behave in certain ways and that if he or she succeeds there will be an agreed reward in which parents may be involved. Discussion with parents about what they feel causes unsatisfactory behaviour may also be helpful and some agreement can be made about a programme which is shared between home and school. It may be that the child would be less troublesome with a different teacher, although it may not be realistic to move him or her in a small school. Particular activities may be the cause of misbehaviour or frustration at inability to achieve. This brings us back to the need to devise appropriate learning programmes.

Primary schools also need to take personal and social education seriously. Gross (1993) suggests:

> In class, all the children are involved in a planned programme of personal and social education lessons; they learn how to recognise and express feelings, how to listen to others, how to resolve conflicts, how to be a good friend, how to keep themselves safe. In addition there are many informal opportunities for children to express feelings and worries to people who will listen.
>
> (Gross 1993: 108)

She also suggests that schools which create an emotionally supportive framework value children's attempts to care for and help each other, and that adults provide examples of respect and empathy, giving children confidence to handle their difficulties, helping them to think out solutions to their problems and building self-esteem.

WITHDRAWN BEHAVIOUR

A quite different set of problems is posed by children who are withdrawn or autistic. Chazan et al. (1980) discovered that teachers generally found it difficult to respond to withdrawn children. They lacked the time necessary to offer the individual help they felt the children needed and it was easy to overlook such children. Many teachers hoped that the normal programme would meet the child's needs.

Wing (1976) describes the characteristics of autistic children as follows:

- a profound lack of affective contact with other people
- an anxiously obsessive desire for the preservation of sameness
- a fascination for objects which are handled with skill and fine motor movements
- mutism, or a kind of language that does not seem to be intended to serve inter-personal communication
- the retention of an intelligent and pensive physiognomy and good cognitive potential, manifested in those who can speak, by feats of memory, and in the mute children, by their skill on performance tests.

(Wing 1976: 15)

She goes on to make the point that not all definitions apply to all children and all circumstances. The item on good cognitive potential is not always present, for example, and there are different degrees of autism.

Autistic children may have problems in understanding speech and have an immature grasp of grammatical structure and confusion over the use of pronouns. Their control of pitch and volume of speech may be poor. Ricks and Wing (1976) describe the speech of some autistic children as follows:

> Vocal delivery tends to be jerky, with poor control of pitch and volume and odd intonation. In consequence, little information is carried by the sound of the voice. Some autistic children have speech that resembles that of children who are congenitally deaf. Facial expression, hand movements and bodily posture are not used to accompany speech as they are in normal people.
>
> (Ricks and Wing 1976: 106)

It may be necessary to teach motor skills by guiding the child's hand rather than by explanation.

Taylor (1976) makes the following points about the problem of teaching autistic children:

> The autistic child's memories appear to be tied up in fixed associations and are not retrievable in the flexible way enjoyed by normal children. They are not available for building complex schemata, making analogies, seeing and making jokes, understanding or using figures of speech or for pretending or inventing.
>
> (Taylor 1976: 206)

Taylor also suggests that the best course is to start with what the child can do, however limited this may be and 'gradually extend the scope of the tasks which are small enough for him to surmount with some effort but without distress' (ibid.: 213). She stresses the value of games such as Ludo which involve working to rules and taking turns with other people. These children will have difficulty in concentrating for any length of time and need tasks which make them think but can also be performed in a short space of time. Keeping a record of the achievement of targets may help to build self-esteem. Behaviour modification can be used with these children and it is valuable if plans are shared between home and school.

It may also be helpful to work at building up the child's self-esteem. Adults in the school can be encouraged to look for something positive to comment on. The child can be given responsibility if he or she is able to do this or asked to act as tutor to someone else. The teacher can make a special point of noticing and praising him or her.

ISSUES FOR CONSIDERATION

- Are we building self-esteem in children with emotional and behavioural problems?
- Are we doing enough teaching of social skills?
- What positive things are we doing to reinforce desirable behaviour?
- How much positive reinforcement of good behaviour do children with emotional and behavioural problems actually get?
- Are we happy with our behaviour policy? Does it provide us with a framework for firm and positive discipline?
- Have we appropriate approaches to learning for children who pose behavioural problems?
- How do we show children who pose behavioural problems that we care about them?
- Do we support each other in dealing with children with behavioural problems?
- Are we doing enough to help children with behavioural problems to put these problems into words?
- Do we give children the opportunity to discuss feelings as part of our ordinary work?
- Have we sufficient counselling skills? Do we use counselling sufficiently?
- Do we know enough about the background of children who pose behavioural problems?
- Do we know how these children view school and their own problems?
- Have we tried behaviour modification? How do we feel about this approach?
- How do we deal with bullying?
- Have children's behavioural problems been discussed with their parents?
- What are we doing about any withdrawn children we have?

Chapter 7

Physical disabilities

The term 'physical disabilities' covers a wide range of conditions, from the child who suffers from a mild degree of clumsiness to the child who is in a wheelchair and needs help with most aspects of daily living. It also includes children with visual and hearing impairment and some physical disabilities also involve difficulties with language. In many cases there will be limitations on the degree of interaction with the environment that is possible, including interaction with other people. This is something the teacher has to try to overcome as far as possible.

Many physical disabilities are easy to recognise and people with such disabilities may have difficulty in getting other people to treat them in a normal way. The fact that someone is sitting in a wheelchair while others are standing creates a difference which has to be overcome. Teachers need to be particularly aware of this problem and to be open-minded about what the child in question is able to do. The goal should always be the maximum independence possible.

Most schools which take in children who are physically handicapped and not mobile will have had some modifications to the building to make their integration possible. Stairs obviously create a problem for children in wheelchairs and ramps are needed for short flights. Even where there is a lift there is a need to consider what such children should do in the event of fire. There will be a need too for special toilet facilities and space for therapies of various kinds and other specialist visits.

In the classroom furniture must be arranged so that a child with physical disabilities can move around easily. Many such children need to move as much as they can in order to improve their mobility. Desks and chairs need to be the proper height for the child and individual children may need a sloping surface for writing. In Chapter 6 quiet areas were suggested for children with emotional and behavioural problems. Some children with physical disabilities, particularly those with cerebral palsy, also work better in a quiet place.

These children may also need special conditions to enable them to take part in subjects like science. They may have difficulty in writing and need longer than other children to achieve similar results. It may also be exceptionally tiring for them and it may be helpful if they can learn to type at a fairly early stage. Some may need a computer which can be operated with the head or the mouth.

Tingle (1990) suggests that 'ideally, when a school plans to admit a child with a physical difficulty, a member of staff, together with the child's potential peer group, should attempt to assume his particular problems and survey the school in advance of his arrival' (p.53). This would seem to be a good way of helping other children to become sensitive to the problems such a child may have in adjusting to the school building.

Children with physical disabilities have to learn to accept them and the school needs to support them in this. Howarth (1987) notes the following about this problem:

> If his handicap is not accepted the child may develop a guilt complex, and view his handicap as a punishment, or turn aggressive against his environment because of fear and anxiety. In contrast, over-protective attitudes may well result in physically handicapped children finding refuge in their disability, and failing to achieve and perform to their maximum potential.
>
> (Howarth 1987: 4)

Some children with physical problems may have had little opportunity to be with their peer group if they have spent a great deal of time in hospital. They may need help in recognising what makes them acceptable to other children. They may benefit from having normal behaviour to copy and from discipline demands made on them as part of a normal class.

It is important when a child with physical disabilities is admitted to a school that staff are given full information about him or her and about the disability and its implications for the child's education. It is also important that the school has a full list from the parents of medical and personal needs together with their telephone number, that of the child's doctor, the name of the hospital in which s/he has been treated and the consultant. It is useful in an emergency if the school knows the child's hospital registration number so that case notes can easily be found. The school will need to know about the drugs the child is taking and what to do if something goes wrong, such as an epileptic fit or difficulty in breathing in the case of asthma. In some cases, such as asthma, older children can be expected to know what to do themselves and have the necessary remedies at hand but teachers of younger children may need to help the child to deal with a particular condition.

Some physically handicapped children will be incontinent and teachers in mainstream schools may feel that this might be a difficulty.

Howarth (1987) in her survey found that this did not pose a problem. 'The majority of incontinent pupils were able to deal, quite independently, with this problem, and the incontinence was generally controlled by daily routine management or by the use of various appliances, following appropriate surgery' (p.142).

If children with physical impairments are to take part in as much of the curriculum as possible, they will need to be included in visits and journeys and this will involve making special arrangements for them. Any necessary drugs or inhalers need to be taken on the journey and arrangements made for children in wheelchairs. It may be a good idea if one of the child's parents is willing to accompany the child on the trip so that they can be satisfied that he or she is being looked after. This will also reduce the pressure on the teacher because the parents can help the child and perhaps other children with the work to be done on the visit. Alternatively an ancillary helper who normally works with the child can come on the visit to take care of him or her.

Many physical disabilities involve a poor kinaesthetic sense so that the child does not have the usual facility for remembering movement. This means that the teacher needs to give lots of structured practice starting with what the child can do so that he or she feels some confidence and gradually moving on to what needs to be learned. This kind of disability makes handwriting very difficult and it may be that a laptop computer will make things easier once the child has learned to type sufficiently. This will mean that work will be on single sheets of paper rather than in an exercise book and the child will need a loose leaf file.

Some of these conditions will be known before the child starts school and the child may come to the school with provision for a care assistant to help with toileting and caring for the child and helping him or her with work in the classroom. The teacher will need to work not only with the care assistant, but also with the physiotherapist, the occupational therapist and perhaps the speech therapist, all of whom may have a contribution to make to helping the child.

In other cases, the problems will gradually reveal themselves as the reception class or nursery teacher observes the children, noting such things as concentration span, language and concept development, laterality and skill in the various tasks which are provided.

Sewell (1991) notes that it is easy to underestimate the potential of disabled people, particularly if they have communication problems.

We can be tempted to provide learning experiences which are too simple, which do not offer cognitive challenge, which do not require the learner to 'struggle' to gain a deeper level of understanding, and which thereby fail to stimulate cognitive growth.

(Sewell 1991: 86)

Bennett *et al.* (1984), in a study which looked at the match of work to children in primary schools, found that 40 per cent of tasks assigned to high attainers underestimated their ability and 4 per cent of tasks assigned to low attainers overestimated theirs.

Many physical disabilities can be helped by the use of computers. Sewell (1991) describes the contribution computers might make as follows:

> A unifying feature of many handicapping conditions concerns the extent to which active control (over the environment) is restricted, both by the nature of the impairment and, in many cases, by the surrounding environment which may impose passivity on an individual. For such individuals, rather than integral components of everyday life, interaction and communication become sources of difficulty and anxiety – often things to avoid rather than seek out. Within this field modern technology, and particularly microcomputers, can be seen as an 'enabling' technology in that it can reduce many of the demands and restrictions placed upon impaired individuals, freeing them for other activities. Frequently this 'enablement' is perceived in the context of improved prostheses – such as scanning devices, mobility aids, input devices and control switches – which make it possible for a disabled individual to interact more fully with the environment and to demonstrate skills which would otherwise have been 'trapped' by the nature of the impairment.
>
> (Sewell 1991: 83)

PARTICULAR DISABILITIES

As increasing numbers of schools start to integrate children who would formerly have been in special schools, teachers need to know about the more common forms of impairment with which they may have to deal. Ideally, when the decision is taken to integrate such children there should be in-service provision for the teachers involved so that they come to the problems with a background of knowledge. There should also be opportunities for the teacher to discuss the child's limitations not only with the parents but also with the school doctor or nurse.

There are also a number of conditions such as asthma which are not immediately evident but which the teacher needs to be aware of. These may have minimal effect on work in the classroom but may involve dealing with the condition from time to time.

Asthma

Asthma is becoming increasingly common and teachers need to know how to deal with attacks. It is a disorder in which the patient has difficulty in breathing. It can be brought on by a number of things including psychological states such as anxiety or excitement, by an allergic reaction to such things as dust, pollen, animal hair, by cold and exercise and so on. Children who suffer from it need to have an inhaler available and to use it when they feel an attack coming on. Teachers should consult with parents about the particular problems of the individual child.

Cerebral palsy

This is caused by various malfunctions of the brain or damage to those parts of the brain which control movement. It may affect vision, hearing and perceptual ability. More common symptoms are lack of balance, jerky and uncontrolled movements and convulsions. Some children will also suffer from epilepsy. There may also be mental retardation, though some children with cerebral palsy may be of normal or above average intelligence. Treatment is through drugs, physiotherapy, speech therapy, bracing and orthopaedic surgery. There is no cure but it is not a progressive condition.

It will be helpful to discuss with the parents what the child is able to do so that the teacher can start from this base. Teachers will find it helpful to talk with teachers from special schools who have had experience of teaching such children. It will also be important to work closely with other disciplines such as speech therapy and physiotherapy.

Clumsiness

Many of the conditions described here affect children's motor skills. There are also some children for whom clumsiness is a major problem. They will have difficulty in writing, find physical education a problem and may be messy eaters. There is a tendency to regard such children as taking insufficient care and of low ability, but they may be unable to help their clumsiness and if they are not given help it may persist. They may also be more intelligent than is at first apparent.

Teachers need to observe these children carefully, looking for the things they find difficult. Do they hold their pencils in the normal way? What are their attempts at drawing and writing like? How do they get on in dressing and undressing for physical education? Can they manage a knife and fork at lunch-time?

Parents may well do things for them in order to get them done, rather than giving the child practice. Such children will also tend to avoid those things they find difficult. It is therefore important that the teacher sees that they practise the tasks they find difficult until they can do them easily. This may mean breaking some of them down into smaller steps.

They may need to practise writing patterns, for example. Tasks like catching a ball may need to be broken down into watching the ball, moving to where it is likely to come, placing the hands ready to catch and moving them so as to have them ready for the ball. These children need plenty of praise when they get things right and not too much blame if they are to develop positive self-images and confidence to try new tasks.

Diabetes

This is an inherited condition, a disorder of the way the body regulates sugar in the blood stream. The hormone insulin, which is necessary for energy to be released from glucose, is normally produced by the pancreas, but this does not happen with diabetics, and the patient may need daily injections of insulin. Regular meals are important and if the child is late for a meal or takes excessive exercise the level of blood sugar may drop and the child may complain of headaches, giddiness or sickness. This can be dealt with by giving him or her fruit juice with added sugar. If too little insulin has been taken the blood sugar level will be too high and the child may complain of tiredness, abnormal thirst and hunger and a need to urinate frequently. This is fairly rare but needs to be treated quickly because it will lead to a coma if not dealt with as an emergency and result in the child being taken to hospital.

It is also important to note that variations in the level of blood sugar may create fluctuations in responsiveness and alertness.

Epilepsy

Epilepsy is a brain disorder which results in small or large seizures. Absence seizures (traditionally called *petit mal*) result in momentary losses of consciousness and these will probably not be noticed and appear to be simply a loss of attention. The traditional *grand mal* seizures, however, involve an extended loss of consciousness in which the child may show convulsive movements and froth at the mouth. These seizures may be controlled by drugs in the majority of cases. An attack may be precipitated by failure to take the drugs at the proper time, by stress or tiredness or by flickering lights.

Treatment is to loosen clothing at the neck and to place something between the teeth since patients sometimes bite their tongues in this situation. A seizure will be frightening for other children and the teacher needs to act calmly until the child recovers. To a large extent epilepsy is controlled by drugs, but there is still a certain hesitation on the part of parents to tell the school that a child suffers from it so that a seizure may come unexpectedly.

Epileptic children may have problems in concentration which affect their learning. 'Absence' seizures may result in a child missing important points in learning which may lead the teacher to think that he or she lacks concentration. Otherwise the child may be regarded as a normal learner.

Hearing impairment

The study by Lyons (1986), which describes the integration of hearing impaired children into mainstream schools, found that the integration of these pupils was not easy. Much depended upon the severity of the disability and the level of language the child had been able to develop. This depends upon the age of the onset of deafness.

Wood *et al.* (1986) comment that

> Deaf children, throughout their development, are likely to experience an increasing gap between what they know, think and feel on the one hand and what they can express, negotiate and communicate about on the other. This growing gap between knowledge and communication often dislocates processes of social interaction.
>
> (Wood *et al.* 1986: 7)

Children who are born deaf have a problem in relating words to what they perceive. This affects their thought processes which may be different from those of hearing people. They may also have difficulty with words such as pronouns. Conversation will be important for their learning. They have to learn to take turns in a two-person conversation. Wood *et al.* comment that

> children not only have to learn to make intelligible sounds and acquire the rules of syntax, but to be meaningful, they also have to discover how to work out the needs of a listener, monitor his understanding, diagnose the nature of any misunderstandings and find ways of establishing mutual comprehension.
>
> (Wood *et al.* 1986: 88)

Lyons (1986) found that the ability of teachers to deal with children with hearing problems depended a good deal on how much they knew about deafness. She also found that although some expressed themselves happy to have such children in their classes they made little effort to modify their practice. They were not always aware of ways in which they could make things easier for a child with a hearing problem. They also had unrealistic ideas about what lip-reading and hearing aids could do.

Although the possibilities of lip-reading are limited because some sounds look the same and others are not really visible, hearing-impaired children rely a good deal on watching the teacher's face and lips for their understanding. It is therefore important to turn towards them when speaking. The teacher's gestures and facial expressions will also be important in helping them to understand.

A teacher who continues to talk and write on the blackboard at the same time will pose problems for these children. They will also find it difficult to look at something on their tables and listen to the teacher at the same time. They need to sit near the front and in good view of the teacher. Classroom discussion will also be difficult because they will not always be able to see the speaker's face, but the teacher can help by repeating contributions. It also helps if the classroom is arranged for discussion so that speakers can see each other.

The teacher and other children also have the problem of understanding the child's attempts at talking. If there are too many occasions when people do not understand this has a negative effect on the child's attempt to speak.

Another valuable contribution is to alert such children individually and see that they are listening when speaking to them. It also helps to make sure that the whole class is quiet before speaking to the group. With older children it helps to write key words and phrases on the blackboard so that a summary is built up. It is helpful to explain to the other children the needs of a hearing impaired child so that they learn to face him or her when speaking and to speak clearly.

A child who has been deaf from birth will also have speech problems. These may not only be difficulties in producing speech but also limitations in vocabulary and sentence structure, and inaccurate pronunciation and abnormal intonation. There should be specialist support available to help in developing speech and vocabulary and sentence structure. These will also be helped by reading. Teachers need to be ready for the problems these difficulties pose and aware that such children's understanding of language may be well below the level that is normal for the age group.

Hearing impaired children are likely to be dependent on hearing aids and function badly without them. Some will want to disguise their need for such aids and the teacher needs to be on the look-out for this, checking that the aid is working and being used.

Spina bifida

This is a defect in which one or more vertebral segments are not joined together. There are three variations of the condition:

- Spina bifida occulta in which the backmost arches of the spine fail to form.
- Meningocele in which there is a protruding sac containing the coverings of the spinal cord.

• Myelomeningocele in which the spinal cord is contained in the protruding sac.

The last two require an operation to prevent infection. Where the spinal cord is involved, the child's legs may be paralysed and he or she may be incontinent. The skin does not respond to pain, heat or touch and care has to be taken that the child does not get pressure sores if he or she is in a wheelchair. Children have to learn to look for skin damage. However, some children may be able to walk with callipers and crutches.

Spina bifida is commonly found with hydrocephalus. This is caused by an increase of spinal fluid within the skull which can cause brain damage. If it is not corrected quickly after birth it will cause mental handicap and possibly paralysis of lower limbs and epilepsy. The head will be abnormally large if the case is severe and the eyes may squint. It is treated by inserting a shunt which drains off the excess fluid into the bloodstream. This operation will need to be repeated as the child grows.

Dealing with such children in school will depend upon the severity of the condition and it will be important for teachers to discuss with parents and with the school nurse or doctor what can be expected from a child with this disability.

Visual impairment

Children with very poor sight pose a different set of problems for the teacher. Spodek *et al.* (1983) note that there are three types of visual impairment which teachers in mainstream schools are likely to encounter:

• impairment of visual acuity which results in objects being seen less clearly than would be the case with a normal person;
• impairment of the field of vision, which affects the angle at which one can see; and
• impairment of colour vision, which results in an inability to distinguish between certain colours.

(Spodek *et al.* 1983: 19)

Those who are integrated into mainstream classes are likely to have some vision and need to make the most of this. A child may have myopic or near-sighted vision so that he or she can see a book but not the board; or, alternatively, far-sighted vision in which the reverse is the case. With the help of low vision aids, the use of a tape-recorder, large print books and worksheets and perhaps a laptop, children who are visually impaired may be able to work well in a normal class.

Children who are blind or have very poor sight have different concepts of the world around them from fully sighted children because their experience is more limited. Jamieson *et al.* (1977) describe this as follows:

Those with normal sight, take in vast amounts of information through their eyes. In day-to-day functioning the world appears to them as structured and unchanging; it is recognisable and verifiable. Close and distant views, colours and physical features, can be examined either intensively or merely glanced at casually; complex relationships can be built up between them. Expressions and movements can be imitated. However, to those with severe interference with vision, none of this can be taken for granted. . . . The visually impaired child may need deliberately to be taught how to analyse and think about his or her environment and encouraged to explore it.

(Jamieson *et al.* 1977: 15)

Visually impaired children make contact with their environment through hearing, smell and touch, and since some things are inaccessible to touch (distant views, fire and other dangerous things) and some, such as colour, are very difficult to explain, their picture of the world is limited. They are also barred from learning by imitation except verbally and do not have the chance to learn the facial expressions and gestures with which we normally accompany speech. They may also have acquired unusual gestures and expressions and need to be helped to avoid these so that they are socially acceptable. All this has to be taught. They may also have been over-protected by parents and not learned to do things for themselves such as dressing and undressing. Words may not have quite the same meaning for them as for other children. Shape concepts will be important and the teacher may be able to use this, providing opportunities to handle things as much as possible. Writing may pose a problem and it may be helpful if these children can learn to type. Those who have no sight at all or whose sight is deteriorating will need to learn braille.

Lowenfeld (1974) suggests that since children with very limited sight may not have had the same degree of experience of playing with toys and manipulating things as sighted children, they may be retarded in their control of their hands and fingers. He also points out that language may be limited at school entry because experience is more limited. This suggests that opportunities for a variety of experiences in which it is possible to examine things by touch are important.

Such children need very good light for all their work and may need an individual reading lamp and low vision aids. They will also need to sit near the board and may need another child to read what is written on it. White boards are easier for visually impaired children to read than blackboards. They may also have difficulty in coping with duplicated worksheets or books with normal sized print and it may be necessary to provide large print books and worksheets. They are likely to be slower than other pupils in looking at pictures or other visual resources. They will have particular problems in practical subjects and will need close supervision in a subject like science. It may help if they can have a partner who will support them. Mobility is important and they should be helped to do as much as possible in physical education. An important aim for these children, as for all children with disabilities, is that they should become as independent as possible.

Visually impaired children may need to be familiarised with the layout of the classroom and when any changes are made the teacher needs to introduce the child to these so that he or she can move about the room easily. The teacher should be careful not to stand against the light.

It is important not to underestimate what such children can do. Many will be intelligent and keen to be regarded as normal people and teachers should try to have high expectations for them while remaining sympathetic to the problems they have.

Defects in colour vision, particularly the green/red confusion, are fairly common and teachers should be alert for children who confuse colours or appear to be selecting coloured equipment by something other than the colour. If there are children with defective colour vision in the class they may need additional clues for selecting anything which is colour coded.

Some children with defective sight may also be reluctant to wear their glasses or use any other aids provided for them and the teacher needs to encourage them to use these.

Jamieson *et al.* (1977) list the following ways in which teachers may need to change their approaches to accommodate such children in their classes:

- reduced use of the blackboard
- a corresponding greater reliance on individual worksheets
- more teacher verbalisation
- wider use of group discussion
- particular emphasis on questioning integrated pupils to ensure that they are following and understanding lesson material
- providing pupils with their own copies of notes
- enlarging maps and diagrams
- allowing them to receive the assistance of peers on certain tasks e.g. copying up notes or undertaking practical experiments
- providing large print materials
- cooperating in the tape-recording of lesson material
- keeping an unobtrusive watch on their progress.

(Jamieson *et al.* 1977: 187)

Other conditions

There are numerous other physical conditions which teachers may encounter from time to time. Many will have little effect on work in the classroom, though they may affect the child's participation in physical education and what he or she is able to do in the playground. In all cases teachers need to consult with parents and the school doctor or nurse about what a child with physical disabilities can safely do.

ISSUES FOR CONSIDERATION

- Are we doing enough to enable children with special needs to become independent?
- Does our building pose any problems to children with physical disabilities?
- What happens to children with physical disabilities in case of fire?
- Is our classroom furniture suitable for children with physical disabilities?
- Do other children understand the problems of children with physical disabilities and can they help them sensibly?
- Are teachers sufficiently knowledgeable about the nature of the physical disabilities of any children in their classes and the implications for teaching and learning?
- Have we all the information we need about such children?
- Are children with physical disabilities joining in as much of the programme as possible, including school journeys and visits?
- Do teachers have a chance to compare notes about children and to learn from external specialists such as physiotherapists and speech therapists?
- Do we underestimate children with physical disabilities?
- Could we use information technology more to help children with physical disabilities?
- Is there other equipment we could be using to help these children?

Chapter 8

The exceptionally able child

DEFINITIONS

It has already been suggested that from the practical point of view, a child might be regarded as having special needs on account of exceptional ability if that child is far in advance of the rest of the class in the work he or she is capable of doing. It may be helpful, however, to consider some of the definitions used more widely and in research. Ogilvie (1973), for example, defines giftedness as follows:

> The term 'gifted' is used to indicate any child who is outstanding in either a general or specific ability, in a relatively broad or narrow field of endeavour. . . . Where generally recognised tests exist as (say) in the case of 'intelligence' then giftedness would be defined by test scores. Where no recognised tests exist it can be assumed that the subjective opinions of originality and imagination displayed would be the criterion we have in mind.
>
> (Ogilvie 1973: 6)

Freeman (1979) took as the definition for her research an IQ score of 140, which is a generally accepted definition. She also comments: 'To be gifted implies potential; achievement is the realisation of potential. We cannot measure potential as such, but only measure achievement and judge potential from that' (p.1).

Hoyle and Wilks (1974) suggests that are three parameters of giftedness: general intelligence, special abilities and creativity.

Gifted children constitute a very varied group including some who have all-round ability, some who have ability in particular aspects of the curriculum, some who are exceptionally creative and some who have exceptional social skills. A child may have very good ability in one area of work and only adequate ability in another. If he or she is in a school where children are streamed by ability as opposed to setted or placed in mixed ability groups, and is placed in a low stream on the basis of general ability, there is a good chance that his or her particular gifts may not be revealed.

Teachers often believe that such children will find their own level, but research (Denton and Postlethwaite 1985) suggests that this is not so and that some children disguise their abilities in order to appear like their peer group. Marjoram (1988) makes the following comments about this:

> There are those who either will not or cannot reveal their potential or their needs in formal situations or examination conditions but when challenged, or relaxed, or involved in some absorbing interest will reveal that freshness, power and originality of their work which tests could not reveal.
>
> Identification has frequently occurred as a result of a sudden flash of insight, a highly idiosyncratic solution to a problem or an arresting piece of work which breaks all the rules.... They happen when variety of opportunity enables them to occur and when the observant teacher notices them and follows them up.
>
> (Marjoram 1988: 28, 29)

Some children will need particular situations to demonstrate their ability which may not be available until later. For example, a brilliant linguist will not reveal his or her gifts in the primary school because foreign languages are not usually taught at this stage, although there may be evidence of strong ability in English and an interest in words. A child may become a first-class violinist but first needs a chance to play the violin. The breadth of the National Curriculum is helpful in giving children many opportunities to develop interests in a range of subjects. What they need is the opportunity to go as far as their interests will take them. This may not necessarily be movement towards the next stage of the National Curriculum but an enrichment of the stage they are at. They are likely to learn quickly and so have more time to pursue interests.

ATTITUDES TO GIFTEDNESS

Attitudes to giftedness have gradually been changing, but those who have researched in this area have found that in the past teachers and headteachers often tend to be doubtful about identifying children as gifted. For example, Ogilvie (1973) received the following comments:

> It is contrary to our philosophy for us to seek to define a category or categories of gifted children. Our primary schools are so organised that we try to provide for the needs of individual children whatever their gifts.

> I am personally extremely doubtful about the wisdom of special provision for gifted children except ... where some particular skill is involved.
>
> (Ogilvie 1973: 4)

Freeman (1979) found that her request to conduct research into gift-edness was seen by some headteachers as 'a form of middle class academic interference' (p.13).

Maltby (1984) encountered the view that resources should go to the underprivileged rather than the gifted who tend to come from middle-class homes.

The counter-arguments are that very able children are important for our future and that a philosophy which suggests that the abilities of every child should be developed as far as possible within the limitations of the school organisation and curriculum implies that gifted children have a special need for development which takes them beyond the general levels of the group they are with.

There are problems about labelling children, however, which, as we have seen, apply to all those with special needs. Once a child is labelled as gifted or posing problems of behaviour or a slow learner, it creates expectations in the minds of teachers which determine in some respects how he or she is treated. Freeman (1979), for example, found that: 'The gifted child may frequently be told at school how much is expected of him; added to his parents' explicit high expectation, the burden of being gifted may become intolerable' (p.126).

Kerry (1983) suggests that labelling a child as gifted 'is very likely to alter the child's self-concept ... whether this is good or bad for the individual it will certainly influence his whole life' (p.22).

Teachers may also have strong feelings about the gifted children in their classes. Greenhalgh (1994) lists some of these feelings as follows:

- resentment at feeling you should do extra work to produce extension activities
- feeling threatened by pupils' superior intellect and/or verbal challenges
- stimulated by the intellectual challenge and curiosity of the pupils
- feeling guilty because you are not stretching the pupils as much as you might be
- finding it difficult to understand pupils who are creative in unorthodox or obscure ways
- envy that your own talents are not as well developed as those of your pupils
- anxious about not knowing what to do to meet the pupils' development needs
- protective about pupils coming over as different from their peers
- pleased that pupils share your strong enthusiasm for your subject
- bewilderment at the pupils' erratic motivation patterns, despite their ability to do the work
- admiration for the pupils' accomplished achievements

- feeling sorry for the pupils because of their relationships with their peers
- concerned because although the pupils seem intellectually gifted they do not seem to be coping emotionally.

(Greenhalgh 1994: 248; with acknowledgement to
Elizabeth Cowne for her contribution)

CHARACTERISTICS OF GIFTED CHILDREN

It has already been noted that this group of children, like other groups of children with special needs, is extremely varied. However, there would seem to be some characteristics common to many of them. Freeman (1979) studied a group of children whose parents were members of the National Association for Gifted Children (the target group) and compared them with two groups of children in the same classes in their schools, the first group having similar IQs to the target group and the second group being randomly selected. Both the able groups came from homes where the parents were well educated and in high status occupations, where there were books and interest in music and art. The parents of those who were NAGC members took education more seriously than the parents of children in the control groups.

The children in the target group were twice as often first born or only children as children in the control groups. In the view of the parents the children were difficult, particularly sensitive, very emotional and independent, had few friends and such friends as they had were older. They had an extraordinary memory, made excellent progress in school and read widely. They also played more musical instruments and had learned to read early. Both parents and teachers noted that these children had more evidence of stomach complaints, respiratory nervous complaints, speech problems, poor eyesight and poor coordination than other groups of children. They also had more patterns of disturbed sleep.

However, when the children were regrouped so that all the children with high IQs were looked at separately there was no evidence that such children were poorly adjusted. In fact the children with the higher IQs were better adjusted than those with lower IQs. There was a larger proportion of boys than girls who were not well adjusted.

This all suggests that parents who identify their children as gifted may tend to pressurise them and this could lead to poor adjustment. It could be seen as an argument against identifying children as gifted. The answer is probably that we need to try to match the individual needs of all children and in talking with parents try to help them to take a balanced view of their children's abilities.

Tanner (1978) points out that there is no relationship between gifted-ness and physical development, but since many children who are gifted come from higher socio-economic groups where the children tend to be larger, most gifted children are well developed physically.

Young and Tye (1992) suggest that teachers need to make themselves aware of what children do outside school and look at the skills and propensities involved. This may enable them to see and use abilities which may not otherwise be evident.

Kerry (1983) notes that gifted children often have poor handwriting, 'a feature which is usually considered to be due to their very rapid thinking abilities which are far in advance of their writing skills' (p.29). He suggests that this may lead teachers to underestimate their ability, especially in the early years.

He found that most gifted children were at least as conforming as any others and suggests that the children most likely to be missed are quiet conforming girls who do what they are told to do. This is the group which the teacher is most likely to underestimate.

He also found that children who were intellectually gifted were excep-tional in concentration, in memory, in multi-attentiveness, in empathy, in speed of perception and in depth of thought. They were also excep-tional in verbal ability, school progress, perseverance, variety of interests, occupational aspirations and musical ability.

Young and Tye (1992) remind us that:

> No matter how gifted children may be, they are still children and not little adults. They must be educated not only in their gifted abilities and related areas but as children with all the emotional, social, physical and other developing and changing needs of children.
>
> (Young and Tye 1992: 71)

They also stress that such children need the security of a rational discipline and encouragement to develop self-discipline. 'Without self-discipline, potential cannot be realised in the scientific, artistic, athletic, literary or any other field. It is discipline which distinguishes between the professional and the dilettante, between accomplishment and dabbling' (ibid.: 66).

THE NEEDS OF EXCEPTIONALLY ABLE CHILDREN

Hoyle and Wilks (1974) report the findings of a study group of teachers which suggest that the primary needs of gifted children were as follows:

- Contact with their average peers
- Contact with children of comparable levels of ability
- To be stretched and challenged even to the point of experiencing failure and humbling experiences

- To be guided rather than directed through a more academic approach to a greater depth of treatment
- To avoid being set apart but to have opportunity to set self apart on occasions
- To pass rapidly through elementary stages and use advanced resources
- To pursue their own lines of research
- To be exposed to some form of counselling – and their parents too
- To be treated like other children
- Contact with teachers gifted in similar fields.

(Hoyle and Wilks 1974: 26)

Marjoram (1988) makes the following comment about the needs of gifted children:

If we are to expect work of real quality from very able children we must feed them with rich experiences, with work of quality, supervise their reading with care, assess their work with diligence and show them that there is much to be learnt from great masters and that few new ideas can be spun out of nothing. This means that teachers themselves must continue to read and learn and cultivate their own visions and capability for wonder. . . . Really good work flows from strong support for intellectually nourishing fare, positive intervention and continuous, critical, constructive assessment.

(Marjoram 1988: 61)

He goes on the suggest that there is a need for good problem-solving activities particularly using real life problems. This is something which has already been suggested as valuable for all children, but it is of particular value to the very able who need to have their thinking challenged. A task such as writing a handbook for new children coming into the school and their parents would involve finding out what new children wanted to know and putting it together in a form that would be attractive to them. It would be important that the work was really intended for use, however, although it might be modified by teachers.

In one school, some very able children were set the task of finding out why there was so much waste at lunch-time. This involved assessing the level of waste and interviewing children to find out why they left food and what could be done about it.

Another task which could be given to a group of such children would be the arrangements for a school journey. This would involve finding out how to get to the agreed destination, its cost, writing letters to make arrangements where necessary and planning how the day should go.

All these tasks would require good supervision by teachers but have within them a discipline and a challenge for getting the detail right which is lacking in invented tasks. A school could collect ideas about tasks which could be given to groups of very able children in this way. Many gifted children will also have ideas of their own about projects which they would like to carry out and these can be incorporated into their work.

Kerry (1983) makes the following comment about independence in learning:

> Clearly bright pupils need independence in learning, encouragement to speculate, the security of psychological climate to ask difficult questions of the teacher and stimulus to work at higher cognitive levels than average or below average pupils. They need to solve problems, and, more significantly, to be encouraged to devise them.
>
> Because of their high ability bright pupils may need some specific social skills too. They need to compete, to be failures and learn to cope with failure. This should help them to develop powers of discrimination and self-criticism.
>
> (Kerry 1983: 88)

He also stresses the importance of bright pupils developing study skills and study habits.

The following study skills are needed if children are to learn independently. Ability to:

- plan a project or an enquiry;
- make judgements and hypotheses about what is planned;
- collect information from a variety of sources including first-hand observation, discussion with other people, and books;
- take notes from observation, discussion and books;
- evaluate the material which has been collected in the light of the original plan or hypothesis;
- select and organise the material which has been collected for presentation in a variety of forms;
- make presentations in various forms such as speech, writing, audio- or video-tape, matching the report to the audience;
- evaluate the presentation.

MAKING PROVISION FOR EXCEPTIONALLY ABLE CHILDREN

Provision for exceptionally able children needs to be of three kinds:

- opportunity to cover the normal curriculum more quickly than other children;
- enrichment of the curriculum, i.e., the provision of work of greater depth and variety;

- extension of curriculum, i.e., the opportunity to go further than others in relation to the same content.

Gifted children, no less than children with learning difficulties, need an individual approach. While they may make a valuable input to initial class discussion when a new topic is introduced, they need work stemming from it which is more demanding than that given to others in the class, just as those with learning difficulties need a version which is less demanding. Sometimes this may be a matter of providing a question which can be dealt with at a variety of levels, so that all children in the class can do something. Sometimes it is a matter of providing tasks at different levels to match the needs of individual children. Very able children may also cover the ground more quickly in subjects such as mathematics which are to some extent linear.

Most aspects of the National Curriculum have within them the possibilities of going further than the majority. Teachers need to look at the possibility of studying particular aspects in greater depth or breadth. This is not necessarily to suggest working at the next stage although this is also a possibility.

The list of needs identified by Hoyle and Wilks (1974) (see pp.123–4) gives a sound basis for considering the provision which should be made for such children. Like other children with special needs they require individual consideration for some of their work. This can be provided either by making special provision or by using open-ended topics which allow the very bright to develop their own ideas. Kerry (1983) suggests that 'Classroom activities should be reviewed to discover to what extent they are likely to tax the able by providing difficulty, complexity, abstractness, economy of thought, goal-relatedness, social value, originality, the need for concentrated effort and persistence' (p.5). One might also add excitement and creating enthusiasm to this list.

There are important decisions to be made by the school if these children are to be given the opportunity to work with others of the same ability for some of the time. It is important for them to learn to live and work with others of lesser ability but they also need the stimulus of other bright children from time to time.

It may be possible to gather a group from different classes in the school to discuss or work on some topic which is in advance of their normal class work. Such a group might read a more difficult book together, work at more difficult mathematical problems, study a more difficult area in science, develop ideas in history or geography or any other idea which teachers can dream up. The group may also have good ideas about areas which they would like to explore. Leyden (1985) suggests that such groups could be inter-school, and this is an opportunity which a number of LEAs have provided.

Where the school is small and there are few very bright children, it may be possible to provide for an individual by drawing on the resources of a nearby secondary school or university and asking if a student of a particular subject which interests the child in question would be prepared to spend some time working with him or her on more advanced ideas. This would need careful arrangement and agreement between the student and the teacher, but it is a scheme which has worked well in some schools. Parents and others in the area have also been involved in schemes of this kind and in one area children identified as gifted have been given a mentor drawn from local people or from students. The mentors have worked with the children individually, taking their thinking on from the stage they had reached. This is particularly valuable when a child has a strong interest in some special topic.

There have also been successful schemes where the individual child has joined up with an older group or spent time in a secondary school for some work.

There is also a case for finding ways of limiting the amount of routine work such children need to do. It is very easy for a busy teacher to deal with children who finish quickly by giving them more of the same. This is not a good solution. Able children should not need to practise work they already know but rather should be spending time on work which is more demanding. It is probably a good idea for such children to have special projects.

Teachers also need to think about the questions they ask in class and check on the number of questions which demand thinking as distinct from recall. Questions which demand thinking and ideas may well elicit ideas from less able children as well as from the able, whereas recall questions, while necessary to check learning, often pose problems for the less able.

Very able children need to develop skills in assessing their own work. Discussion about a piece of work with the teacher should start with the teacher asking the child what he or she thinks about it so that the child gets into the habit of assessing his or her work. Children may also profitably assess each other's work, working in pairs and talking about how it could be improved.

The advantages of collaborative group work have already been discussed. This has much to offer very able children and they have much to contribute.

Young and Tye (1992) make the following point about structuring learning:

> With bright, keen young children, their curiosity and eagerness to master new skills may need little stimulation if they see the relevance of what they are required to do. For all children need to see pattern

and structure in what they are learning, whether it be a skill or an intellectual task.

(Young and Tye 1992: 84)

Maltby (1984) perhaps sums up the message which teachers need to consider in managing exceptionally able children: 'Gifted children are individuals and therefore provision for each child should be considered according to the individual personality of the child and teacher concerned. There is no correct way to provide for gifted children, only a way for each child' (p.209).

DEALING WITH EXCEPTIONAL ABILITY IN DIFFERENT SUBJECT AREAS

Art and craft

The child who is exceptionally able in this area will be drawing at a level well beyond the normal for his or her age group. There may be a good deal of detail, attempts at showing a third dimension, placing things so that they overlap in a picture, inventive and unusual ideas, marked enthusiasm for drawing and painting and for all art and craft activities.

Ability to copy or draw photographically at an early age does not necessarily indicate high ability unless accompanied by evidence of original thinking and inventiveness.

Freeman (1979) describes the children gifted in this area as follows:

Children gifted in fine art are constantly concerned with visual presentation, attempting to record the images they see. Their presentations are illuminating and revealing; they bear the imprint of the artist, both in emphasis and in relationships between colours and shapes. As well as mastery of the techniques of using their materials, they are sensitive to their aesthetic qualities; this is not the same as learned competence.

(Freeman 1979: 80)

The needs of children with this kind of ability are well provided for in the National Curriculum. They should have the opportunity to explore and become competent in using different media. They need good opportunities for drawing and painting from first-hand experience and the opportunity to study the works of artists and craftsmen both past and present.

Language

Children who are particularly able in language are likely to show skill in using complex language, give evidence of a wide vocabulary, have fluent speech and ability to match language to audience or readership at an early age. They will probably use imagery, write well in different forms such as stories and poems and plays as well as straightforward accounts when these are required. They are likely to have the ability to create a mood, develop an idea or sustain an argument. They will be sensitive to literature and enthusiastic readers.

Marjoram (1988) makes the following points about language ability:

> He or she will gradually learn to use language coolly, judicially and economically when describing an experiment or weighing a situation in history. They will know how and when to express wonder, passion or delight. They will learn to turn a phrase neatly, invent an unusual metaphor, select an appropriate form be it prose or blank verse.
>
> (Marjoram 1988: 89)

Such children need opportunities to write for different audiences and in different forms and to become self-critical about their writing. Some may need to learn to write briefly and economically.

Mathematics

Children who are exceptionally able in mathematics are likely to demonstrate a liking for numbers, skill in using logical connectives, interest in geometrical pattern-making and the use of sophisticated criteria for ordering, sorting and classifying. They will grasp the essence of a problem quickly, relate one problem to another and be able to generalise. Such children will probably be able to skip over intermediate steps in a logical argument and be persistent in searching for the most elegant solution. They will be confident in new mathematical situations and continually pose new problems to themselves.

Freeman (1979) suggests that gifted mathematicians may reveal themselves by 'the original remark, the unexpected question, the leap to the abstract, the distrust of intuition, a persistence and a desire for perfection. They may detect ambiguity or imprecision in the teacher's language' (p.81).

Mathematical ability should not be confused with the ability to perform calculations. Skill in calculation is of considerable value, but a distinction must be made between this more limited talent and a facility for handling abstract numbers imaginatively and with pleasure.

These children need the demands of new sorts of mathematical problems and also problems from real life which do not have neat textbook answers.

Movement

Children gifted in movement might show a level of skill, understanding and appreciation of movement in advance of their age group. They will have complete confidence, determination and stickability in addition to natural economy of movement and the ability to acquire new skills easily. They are likely to have an ability to carry out physical movements with control and quality so that they are aesthetically pleasing to an observer. They will also have a natural talent for complex movement requiring a range of skills such as resilience, mobility, strength and stamina. They will develop games skills easily.

Such children can be encouraged to develop sequences of movement, paired work, skill in dance, and older children will benefit from opportunities to play in team games.

Music

Musically gifted children are likely to be aesthetically responsive and musically alert, open to new musical ideas and imaginative in the use of sound. They will probably have an unusually good musical memory and possess exceptional powers of aural discrimination for their age with regard to pitch, tonal qualities and precise duration of sound.

Freeman (1979) found that all the children in her study who showed musical or fine art talent came from homes where this was a priority.

The National Curriculum requires composition from children at appropriate levels in each Key Stage and this will offer good opportunities for musical children to show their abilities. They also need opportunities to sing in choirs, play in musical ensembles and listen to a variety of kinds of music.

Science

Children who are exceptionally able in science are likely to observe things closely, watching, touching, smelling, be naturally curious and ask interesting questions, be able to describe objects and events accurately. They may use unusual and interesting criteria in sorting objects, show inventiveness in making models, become totally absorbed for long periods of time in something they are watching or working out, try out ideas to see what happens and will often try to work out things for themselves.

Marjoram (1988) suggests that:

Those who are gifted in science can see the relevance of what is learned in science lessons to situations outside the laboratory. They have the capacity to leap ahead or jump steps in an argument and to detect faulty logic, to perceive the direction of an investigation and to anticipate realistic outcomes. They can connect scattered or disparate data into coherent patterns and pursue an investigation persistently until all reasonable avenues have been explored. Many have the ability to hold a problem in the mind and analyse it.

(Marjoram 1988: 118, 119)

Children able in science will benefit when the tasks posed can be carried out at a variety of levels and also when specific tasks are planned for them which make considerable demands upon their ability. They will also benefit from encouragement to pose problems they see in their everyday life.

THE PROBLEMS OF GIFTED CHILDREN

Many very able children have no problems of any note and are as mature socially as they are academically. Others have problems in getting on with their peer group. Freeman (1979), for example, found that children in her target group were described by their parents as difficult to bring up and not very popular with friends or teachers. Some gifted children find their peer group limited and seek friends among older children who may be socially more mature. Others become 'loners'. Teachers can help this in some respects by ensuring that very able children have social skills. In some cases they are too ready to show their peers that they are critical of their slowness and they need to be encouraged to think about how the other person feels when confronted with critical comments of this kind.

Some find that the expectations of parents and teachers cause stress. Such children become afraid to fail and reluctant to try anything new or difficult. Much depends upon the climate in the school. Maltby (1984) says that 'for a child to work obviously in advance of others, he has to be in an environment in which getting ahead is permissible and not one where all the children are required to work at the same pace' (p.65). He or she also needs to be in an environment where children are encouraged to see failure as a normal part of learning.

Callow (1994) suggests that in some cases very able 'children can become deeply troubled by a lack of suitable challenge and become so disruptive as to appear maladjusted' (p.152). This obviously points to the need for differentiation within the classroom which is necessary for all children with special needs. It also shows the need for training independence in learning, organising the classroom to support this and providing encouragement for very able children to pursue studies at a more demanding level.

Another less important problem is that some very able children find handwriting too slow a process for their thoughts and become very untidy writers. This can be helped by ensuring that they are able to form letters and join writing correctly and by giving them the opportunity to use the word processor to produce their work from time to time.

ISSUES FOR CONSIDERATION

- Are we doing enough to identify exceptionally able and gifted children?
- What criteria are we using to identify them?
- Are we making sufficient demands on them?
- How do we feel about regarding them as having special needs?
- How can we avoid the disadvantages which appear to stem from labelling children who have any kind of special need?
- Are we satisfying the parents of very able children that we are meeting their needs?
- Do any of these children need help in relating to their peer group?
- Are we underestimating any children who are quiet and conforming or who have poor handwriting perhaps because they think so quickly?
- Can we provide for these children so that they have some opportunities of being with a group of similar ability from time to time?

Chapter 9

Working with parents

A series of Education Acts over the past ten years has built rights for parents into the education service and the Code of Practice stresses the importance of involving parents. It makes the following statement about partnership with parents:

> Children's progress will be diminished if their parents are not seen as partners in the educational process with unique knowledge and information to impart. Professional help can seldom be wholly effective unless it builds upon parents' capacity to be involved and unless parents consider the professionals take account of what they say and treat their views and anxieties as intrinsically important.
>
> (DFE 1994c: para. 2.28, p.13)

Where children have special needs it is important for parents and teachers to work together so that the demands made on the children are as consistent as possible. This is easy to say, but the pressures of daily life in school often make it difficult to put into practice. It may be helpful to consider the ways in which this cooperation can operate.

INFORMING PARENTS THAT THEIR CHILD HAS SPECIAL NEEDS

Teachers are increasingly conscious of the need to explain what they are doing in the classroom to those outside. In particular they are aware of the need to let parents know how they work and why they work in a particular way. Where a child is not making good progress it is not unusual for the parents to assume that this is the fault of the teacher. The teacher, for his or her part, may assume that it is the fault of the home background. It is only when teachers and parents work together that such myths can be dispelled and both home and school contribute to the child's progress. Greenhalgh (1994) sums up this problem as follows:

Relationships with parents is an area full of possibilities for the development of defence and splitting, with schools and parents potentially
blaming each other for difficult situations which might develop,
thereby inhibiting the capacity for joint work on problem resolution.
This is particularly the case with the parents of children experiencing
emotional and behavioural difficulties, who are likely to have more
than average anxieties about their children.

(Greenhalgh 1994: 293)

If this kind of problem is to be avoided it is wise to talk with parents
of children with special needs at an early stage, sharing with them some
of the school's findings, inviting contribution from them and discussing
what the school is proposing to do and what the parents can do to help.
The class teachers of the younger children will have informal opportunities to talk with parents about problems as they bring and collect their
children to and from school and the school's normal arrangements for
talking to parents and reporting to them should provide opportunities
for alerting parents to the fact that their children are not progressing as
well as the teacher would wish. However, once a decision has been made
to register a child as having special needs a longer meeting should be
arranged to discuss this.

It is important to prepare for this meeting. All the information the
teacher has collected about the child should be available, including
samples of his or her work which demonstrate the special needs the
teacher wishes to draw attention to. It may also be a good idea to have
some work from children of average ability available so that the parents
can see what other children in the class are able to do.

It is also valuable to identify clearly the purpose of the meeting. This
will be first to inform the parents that the teachers are of the opinion
that the child has special needs and to explain to them the school's
programme for dealing with these. It should also involve getting as much
information about the child from the parents as possible, particularly
information about his or her early development and reactions to school.
In addition it is an opportunity to enlist the aid of parents to help the
child at home.

The meeting must involve the classroom teacher who can give chapter
and verse about the progress the child is making. Headteachers need to
decide whether they should be present at such a meeting or whether
the task can be left to the classroom teacher or the special needs coordinator with the classroom teacher. Where the teacher is experienced
and is known to have good relationships with parents the meeting can
be less formal with the teacher dealing with the situation. Where the
teacher is young and inexperienced the headteacher or the special needs
coordinator would be wise to be present, but perhaps should allow the

class teacher to conduct the meeting, helping if problems arise. This might be regarded as a form of in-service training since teachers are not usually trained to deal with parents. There should be discussion before-hand about the ground to be covered and a review of what happened afterwards so that the teacher learns from the experience. It is also important to make a record of such meetings immediately afterwards so that the information is available for the next meeting. It may also be wise to write to the parent after the meeting setting down what has been agreed.

The meeting should involve talking about the strengths the child has as well as his or her problems. Parents will want to know what will happen and who will be involved. They will want to know what they can do, how they will be involved and about the services they can expect.

For their part, parents will know a good deal about how their child reacts to things, what interests and what stimulates him or her and so on. Dolton (1991) reminds us that parents are

> in intimate daily contact with the children and as such can observe the raw behavioural data and may indeed construe and interpret it more accurately than a representative of the education service. Equally they may collude [with] or deny what is apparent to others.
>
> (Dolton 1991: 42)

Spodek *et al.* (1983) also discuss the way parents may see the problems. They may question the expertise of those who are describing the problem. They may feel helpless, frustrated and angry towards the child and themselves. They may feel a sense of guilt that they have caused the problem and they may look for other people to blame. They may also feel ashamed of their child. Parental attitudes are likely to be very complex and teachers discussing the problem with them need to be very sensitive towards their feelings.

On the other hand, parents will know how the child is reacting to school, may be worried about the child's lack of progress and be re-assured by a frank discussion of the problems the child is meeting and the school's plans for overcoming them. For some the information that their child is not progressing well may come as a shock and parents may find the situation difficult to accept. It is in such a context that it will be helpful for an inexperienced teacher to have a more experienced person present.

The teacher needs to establish a friendly, positive atmosphere while at the same time making clear the particular problems the child is experiencing. It is important not to gloss over these in order to make the parents feel happier about the situation, and also to avoid anything which could be construed as educational jargon. The teacher may have to make the case that the child actually does have special needs compared with other children and may also have to do a lot of reassuring that the school, with help from the parents, can do something positive. The teacher should explain carefully what the school is planning to do and suggest ways in which the parents can help. The meeting should end with a summary of what has been agreed.

Many special schools use 'home/school books' in which the teacher records each day what the child has done and the parents record anything relevant which has happened at home. If parents are involved in contributing to the overall programme this is a very helpful device, although it is demanding on the teacher.

Wolfendale (1992a) suggests that schools need to think about how they set the scene for such meetings with parents. The situation should be informal, preferably with everyone in easy chairs so that those involved can relax with each other. The teachers must develop their own listening skills and encourage the parents to talk, demonstrating that they are taking in what the parents are saying by summarising from time to time. They need to be prepared to share their feelings about the situation and encourage parents to do the same. They also need skill in concluding the meeting, generally by summing up and agreeing the action that should stem from it.

THE CONTRIBUTION OF PARENTS TO ASSESSMENT

The Code of Practice speaks of partnership with parents. McConachie (1986) states: 'Partnership seems to imply equality of parents with professionals in defining intervention strengths and goals, recognising the different strengths that each side brings to the partnership and what knowledge and perspective each side lacks' (p.159). Pearson and Lindsay (1986) describe partnership in action:

It is difficult to see that focussing on problems is a viable form of partnership unless parents already feel at home in school, welcomed by the head and other staff, able to make easy contact. On that basis the early worries can be shared, parents involved in home activities to complement those at school, more serious difficulties gradually accepted. Conversely, a summons out of the blue, the discovery that one's child had difficulties one did not suspect, inevitably starts any 'partnership' off badly and the chances are it will never become such, rather a polarised antagonism.

(Pearson and Lindsay 1986: 18)

Mittler and Mittler (1982) list five factors required in partnership:

* mutual respect and the recognition of equality
* the sharing of skills and information
* the process of sharing

- a joint role in decision making
- the recognition of the individuality of families and the uniqueness of the child with special needs.

(Mittler and Mittler 1982: 113)

Wolfendale (1992b) reminds us that parents are assessing their children constantly and that they can therefore contribute information which is not available in other ways and which complements the information that the professionals discover. Parents know their children's likes and dislikes, moods, anxieties and reactions to people and events. She suggests that they will be able to complete developmental skills or behavioural check lists and perhaps create a profile of 'My child at home'.

PARENTS AND INTEGRATION

Schools will have to deal with some situations where children who would not formerly have been in mainstream schools become pupils there. In some cases this will involve a special unit on the school site and the gradual integration of children into some lessons. In other cases it may involve taking in a child or children with considerable problems as part of normal classes. Parents of other children will be apprehensive about this and will need reassuring that this should not mean that their children will lose out because the teacher will need to spend a lot of time with the children with special needs. They are more likely to be reassured if the admission of these children involves the appointment of support teachers or ancillaries with responsibility for their physical care.

The parents of children with serious disabilities have generally been found to welcome the idea that their children should be educated in the mainstream school. It makes them feel that their children are nearer to normality and getting a better preparation for adult life in a non-handicapped community than would be possible in a special school. Howarth (1987) studied the integration of physically handicapped children in primary schools and made the following comment about parents views: 'Parents described normality as an end in itself; the promotion of maturity and personal development; growth in independence; implications for how handicap is viewed and benefits for the parents themselves' (p.33).

Parents will need reassurance, however, that the school can cope with the problems that their child poses. This will not be altogether easy for the staff because they may be uncertain themselves at the early stages of an integration programme that they will be able to cope. They should be prepared to learn from parents about the nature of the disability and what it is possible for the child to do.

The children already in the school will also need preparation for integration, especially if the children joining them have physical disabilities. The teacher should discuss this with them and help them to imagine what it is like to be unable to walk or to find it difficult to do things with their hands or to hear or see. He or she also needs to enlist their support in making the child joining them feel welcome and at home and they should discuss how to do this.

PARENTS AS TEACHERS

Parents normally want to help their child, particularly if the child appears to have difficulty or seems to them to be exceptionally able. Parents are the natural teachers of children and all parents have taught their children many things. This is a source of help which no school can afford to reject and it is seen as part of the Code of Practice which regards parental help at home as part of the Individual Education Plan. Chazan *et al.* (1980) describe the value of this kind of parental involvement:

> When a child realises that his parents and teacher are working together it shows him that his parents are interested and share the aims of his teacher. Parents gain from the relationship by realising that they are able to play a part in their child's education irrespective their own ability.

(Chazon *et al.* 1980: 166)

Some approaches for involving parents with reading have already been discussed in Chapter 5 and there are many more ways in which parents can help. At the nursery and reception class stage parents can help children's language development by reading to them and by discussing everything they do together, by encouraging the child to talk and listening carefully to him or her. In addition to hearing reading, parents can discuss what is being read and discuss pictures in books, play games designed to foster particular skills both in reading and mathematics, use apparatus supplied by the school and the opportunities which occur in everyday life for mathematical practice.

Schools for their part may need to provide workshops for parents so that they can learn how best to help their children. These should be designed to give parents confidence that they are capable of working with their children and should deal with the system of working which the school wishes to set up. There should be good opportunities for discussion and a number of schools have found it a good idea to give a demonstration of the role they want parents to play. In particular the school should stress that praise is important. Children need to feel good about what they are doing and have their self-esteem enhanced.

Where reading is concerned, parents need to know what they should do if a child is unable to read a word and how to make judgements about whether the book is at the right level for the child. Schools will need enough books for children to have a choice of book within their capacity but mistakes will occur in choosing books at an appropriate level.

Schools should develop methods of communicating with parents about what is being done at home in relation to what is being done at school. This is time consuming, but the evidence is that children make considerably better progress in reading, for example, when parents hear reading at home (Topping and Wolfendale 1985).

An important management decision is the extent to which parental help at home is regarded as something for all children or whether it is restricted to children with special needs. It is desirable to encourage all parents to become involved in helping their children, but the scale on which this is needed for children with special needs where the teacher needs to check each day the reading done at home means that it is only possible for a few children in each class. Some of the schools which undertake this practice have a weekly form for parents which the parents complete each day giving information about what the child has read with the parent and any comments the parent may have. The teacher then checks this reading and makes any comments for the parent. This flow of information helps to maintain the system. (The school would also be wise to provide plastic folders for the books to be carried home.)

Where this is the practice for everyone a simpler system needs to be evolved. The school must demonstrate that teachers are aware that parents are helping in this way, perhaps asking parents to record in a similar way to that for children with special needs but responding to a few children's parents only each week.

Schools will also need to decide what to do about children whose parents do not read English and parents who do not wish to be involved. In the case of those whose parents do not read English there may be older siblings who would hear the child read regularly. It may also be possible to set up a system using volunteers from the neighbourhood working with children in school time, or older children might be used.

At the start of a programme the staff are likely to be enthusiastic and share this enthusiasm with the parents. As time goes on the enthusiasm may wane and the contribution of parents may gradually fade away. Wolfendale (1992a) suggests that the following increase the likelihood of a programme lasting:

- commitment
- clearly identified aims
- explicit short term and longer term goals

- mix of 'top-down' and 'bottom-up' decision making
- availability of a range of training strategies
- availability of supporting materials and resources
- regular review points
- periodic evaluation by all participants
- record-keeping that is integral with the programme
- willingness to be flexible and adapt to changing circumstances.

(Wolfendale 1992a: 12)

OTHER PARENT INVOLVEMENT IN SCHOOL

Parental involvement in teaching their children is likely to be most effective where the school involves parents in many ways and parents feel welcome in the school and able to contribute to what happens there. The Code of Practice sees them as contributing to decision-making where children with special needs are concerned and there will be other areas where their views are important in making decisions.

It is valuable if a school has spare space to provide a parents' room where parents who come in to help in various ways can gather and have a cup of coffee. This can be a place for exhibiting books and materials which are being used in school and for displaying other information for parents. This can also provide a space for self-help parent groups to meet and discuss their problems, perhaps with a psychologist or the headteacher.

Class meetings of parents are valuable. At these the teacher talks about the work the class will be doing and how parents can help with it. Parents may also be invited to class assemblies.

In many schools parents are now involved in working with teachers in the classroom and this is particularly valuable where the teacher has children with special needs since the parent, with guidance from the teacher, may be able to give such children individual help for some of their work.

HOME VISITS

Many teachers find visiting the homes of children with special needs very helpful. This is particularly true where the child has serious disabilities. There are considerable advantages in seeing parents in their home environment. Some teachers fear that parents may resent this as an intrusion, but teachers who have undertaken such visits have found that they were made very welcome in people's homes and that parents have very much appreciated the teacher taking the trouble to visit. The teachers have also felt that they have learned a good deal as a result and formed a new and closer relationship with the parents.

COMPLAINTS PROCEDURES

At every stage it is possible that parents will be dissatisfied with what is happening even though the school has taken care to keep them informed and involved. Headteachers are generally practised at dealing with complaints however good their schools, but some complaints may come directly to class teachers and it is important that they are trained to deal with this eventuality.

The important thing in dealing with parental complaints is not to become defensive, to listen carefully and ask questions to be sure that the complaint is what it seems to be. It is not unusual for someone to start complaining about something comparatively trivial, but if the other person listens carefully, it is later revealed that the worry is much more serious and deeper and even about something quite different. Making a trivial complaint may be a way into much more serious concerns.

If the complaint is about something which is genuinely at fault the best reaction is to apologise sincerely and go on to discuss how to put matters right. If it is that the situation has been misunderstood then it is wise to wait until the person complaining has talked him- or herself out and then to suggest that while the view the parent has is understandable, from the teacher's point of view it looks a little different. It is then possible to describe what was intended.

The next stage is to ask the parent how this sort of problem can be avoided in the future and what can be done to meet the points the parent is making. The idea is to remain positive at all stages and to remain apparently calm, avoiding showing any anger which may be felt.

Finally it is wise to record the conversation and possibly write to the parent recording the outcome of the meeting.

This process may not be sufficient to satisfy some parents who may feel that the school has not dealt adequately with their concern. It is therefore necessary to have a complaints procedure which allows parents who are dissatisfied to take the complaint further. It is likely that the first stage will be the parent complaining to the class teacher, although in some cases parents may go directly to the headteacher. If the parent is not satisfied with the class teacher's explanation the headteacher is the next step and class teachers should make it clear to parents complaining that this is a possibility. If parents are still dissatisfied after seeing the headteacher then it should be possible for them to meet a small group of governors to discuss the problem. It is likely that parents who are still dissatisfied at this stage will take the matter to the LEA.

ISSUES FOR CONSIDERATION

- Are we doing enough to introduce the school to parents?
- Do we give parents a sufficient understanding of what the school is trying to do and of their part in it?
- Do we do enough to help parents become more aware of, and interested in, the way they might contribute to the learning of their child?
- How is the school's policy for SEN made available to parents?
- Are our arrangements for informing parents that their child has special needs satisfactory?
- Do we do enough to meet parental concerns whether from parents of children with special needs or others?
- Are parents aware that the school recognises and values the experience they have of their children?
- Do we need to do anything to prepare parents to help their children?
- What part do parents play in the assessment of their children's progress?
- Have we considered the possibility of home visits for children with special needs?
- Have we an adequate complaints procedure?

Chapter 10

Support services

Effective multi-professional work is not easy to achieve. It requires cooperation, collaboration and mutual support. Each professional adviser needs to be aware of the roles of his colleagues and should seek to reach agreement with them on their several roles and functions. It follows from this that his advice should reflect his own concerns leaving others to concentrate on their particular area of expertise.

(DES 1983: para. 34, p.8)

Teachers dealing with children with special needs are likely to have to work with a range of people from the education, health and social services. This is particularly the case where a school is taking children who formerly would have been in special schools. Each of the people involved has his or her particular contribution to make and it is important that the classroom teacher has a chance to talk with them all so that they can exchange information about the children with whom they are concerned. The classroom teacher will want to learn what he or she can from the specialist about the best way of dealing with the problems the particular child is posing. Lacy (1991) suggests that

Success requires careful planning, using regular contacts as a means of achieving a climate of trust and shared expertise. . . . The key issues are effective communication and an understanding of the different roles and working practices of the members of a multi-disciplinary team.

(Lacy 1991: 104)

This is not easy. None of the people concerned has time to spare and each has a different perspective. It is only by meeting together regularly and discussing the individual children for whom they share responsibility that trust can be built up. Howarth (1987), for example, describes how the headteachers and teachers in her survey found that the more they saw of educational psychologists the more value they placed on their contribution. She also found that in general the schools in her study felt that they saw too little of almost all the specialists involved. This is even more likely to be the case now since many services have experienced cuts in provision.

The specialist services which may be involved in working with schools include educational psychologists, advisers and advisory teachers, social workers, the educational welfare officer, speech therapists, occupational therapists and physiotherapists as well as the school nurse and doctor. There will also be specialists in learning difficulties who need to be involved at Stage 3. In some authorities their services are available if schools can afford to buy them, and where this is the case it will be important for the school to define very clearly what they require. Some areas also have an arrangement whereby teachers from a special school or unit visit the local schools to advise on how best to tackle the problems the teachers encounter.

The Audit Commission (1994) notes the various problems existing in getting all the relevant services to work together. The Commission expresses concern about the problems for children with disabilities being educated in mainstream schools and states: 'There were fears of long delays for such children, given the difficulty of providing services to children who were geographically less easy to reach (than those attending special schools)' (p.29). They also note that there was often confusion about which service should provide equipment for children with disabilities.

Galloway (1985) lists the contributions which specialists should be able to make as follows:

- They can provide an independent view of the child's needs. Precisely because they are not working with the child on a day-to-day basis, they should have greater objectivity, and see the child's difficulties from a broader perspective.
- They should have knowledge of good practice in other schools in the LEA and of national trends. This knowledge should enable them to disseminate ideas, and put teachers in touch with colleagues with relevant experience both in special and ordinary schools.
- They should have access to other sources of help, for the school, the child or the family. Further they should be able to advise on the need for more specialised investigation.
- They have specialised training enabling them to contribute to a comprehensive assessment of the child's needs. Since the needs of the children reflect a complex interaction between medical, psychological, educational and social factors that assessment should be multi-disciplinary.

(Galloway 1985: 65)

There is a problem over specialists' contribution in mainstream schools which does not exist in the same way in special schools. In the special school there is usually considerable work for the physiotherapist or the speech therapist. Integration may mean that each school has only a small number of children needing this kind of help and this means more time travelling for the people concerned.

However, much can happen if a school is determined to make it happen, and where the school sets out to work with the other services and makes this a priority those concerned are likely to do their best to respond. In any case at Stage 3 and beyond there is a requirement to involve specialists in learning difficulties and this must be written into the Individual Education Plan.

It is important that teachers regard the specialist services as contributing to their work in the classroom with children with special needs, rather than seeing any particular specialist as taking over responsibility for the child. There is also the problem that the specialist comes at a time convenient for him or her and this may not be a convenient time for the teacher. This may mean that the child with whom the specialist is working misses something important in the classroom which the teacher has to make good at another time. There are many possibilities for misunderstandings and frustrations in the demand that all those concerned with a child work as a team and it is therefore important that the teacher sees him- or herself as the person with major responsibility for the child who attempts, with support from the special needs coordinator, to bring together all the separate pieces of the provision being made.

In many cases, particularly where special needs arise from physical or neurological problems, the initial identification will be made by a medical officer. When the child starts school, parents will have a good deal of information about their child's problems but it is important that a doctor or nurse also informs the headteacher and class teacher about the cause and nature of the child's problems so that they are able to see the implication of these for the child's education. Teachers may have to deal with emergencies such as a child having an asthma attack and it is important that they are aware of what is involved and how to deal with problems which could be life-threatening.

The educational psychologist should be a very important support for the school. He or she should have advice to offer on many of the problems which confront teachers dealing with children with special needs of all kinds, including the very able. This should also be true of the special needs adviser if there is one. Both should be able to advise on organisation, approaches, resources and equipment and educational psychologists have a particular role in assessing children and diagnosing difficulties and advising on how teachers can assess children. They also have a statutory role in the statementing process. The special needs adviser will have a role in in-service work and, together with advisory teachers, may be able to offer the school custom-made in-service provision as well as providing more general courses for teachers.

Many authorities employ advisory teachers for special needs as well as specialists in learning difficulties, some of whom have a responsibility for children with visual or hearing problems. Advisory teachers offer advice to headteachers, coordinators and classroom teachers on many aspects of special needs work and some will work alongside a classroom teacher for a short time helping him or her to develop work. The major responsibility for teachers who are specialists in learning difficulties may be helping small groups and individuals in a group of schools. The Code of Practice sees them helping at Stage 3 and beyond but they may be prepared to offer advice about children at earlier stages.

The physiotherapist will be important to schools where there are children with physical disabilities. They may provide exercise routines for these children and will be able to advise the class teacher on what the child is able to do and his or her level of mobility. Howarth (1987) describes how some physiotherapists working in schools in her survey overcame the problem of the limited amount of physiotherapy time available to them by training ancillary helpers to undertake exercise routines with the children for whom they were responsible.

Schools with children with physical disabilities may also seek advice from occupational therapists who will advise them on how to help children to become more independent in the activities of daily living such as dressing, eating and using the toilet. They should have a particular contribution to make where children with physical disabilities are concerned in advising on how computers can be used to help these children interact with their environment and the way they need to sit to work and to use the computer. They will also be able to advise on other aids and equipment and any necessary adaptations of the buildings.

Speech therapists will be important where the school has children with communication problems. They should not only work with individual children but also advise the classroom teacher on the best way to help them. It is valuable if the speech therapist can sometime work within the classroom and see how the child reacts in the classroom context and what is possible for the teacher.

The school nurse, the educational welfare officer and social workers may all have parts to play in supporting the school with children with special needs. The school nurse will support the doctor in advising on the implications for the teachers of the medical conditions of children. The education welfare officer and other social workers may be able to advise teachers on the implications of any stress the child may be experiencing at home.

Children with physical impairments may well have an ancillary helper allocated to them to help with toileting, medication and supervision at lunch- and break times and also to help them with work in class. They have a particular role in helping the children to become independent. Such children may feel that this makes them different from other children and may be happier if the ancillary helper sometimes helps other children. This would seem to be a good use of time and helpful to the teacher who should discuss and plan with the helper, both for the child in question and for any other help the ancillary may be able to provide. Ancillary helpers need to know a good deal about the problems the child experiences.

Most of these people may have something to offer to the training of class teachers to deal with children with special needs.

ISSUES FOR CONSIDERATION

- Are class teachers making sufficient contact with visiting specialists?
- Are we taking sufficient advantage of the specialist knowledge of those who visit us?
- Do we feel that we are working as a team with visiting specialists?
- Have we solved the problems of professional confidentiality?
- Are we getting the medical information we need?
- Are we getting the psychological advice we need?
- Are we getting advice on the management aspects of special needs?
- Could we make more use of advisory teachers and teachers who are specialists in learning difficulties if they could spare us the time?

Chapter 11

Staff development

The Code of Practice (1994) makes the following statement about in-service provision:

> The school's SEN policy should describe plans for the inservice training and professional development of staff to help them work effectively with pupils with special educational needs. The SEN inservice training policy should be part of the school's development plan and should, where appropriate, cover the needs of non-teaching assistants and other staff. Schools should consider the training needs of the SEN coordinator and how he or she can be equipped to provide training for fellow teachers.
>
> (DFE 1994c: para. 2.26, p.12)

If the school is to maintain good provision for children with special needs, every member of staff needs to acquire the necessary skills and knowledge. This need not be time-consuming if the organisation for special needs is examined, looking at the staff development opportunities it offers. The teacher who acquires the skills to manage a class where there are children with a variety of special needs, including some children with exceptional ability, will be a better teacher of all the children in the class. The aim should be to enable every classroom teacher to become competent at diagnosing and providing for the more common special needs. The skills of classroom teachers will be supported by those of the coordinator who should have a wider range of skills and knowledge.

There may need to be briefing and some in-service training of others besides teachers. Governors will need to be briefed fully about their responsibilities and to consider their implications. Non-teaching staff may have to deal with children with physical or behavioural problems and they may need to be briefed about the children concerned and how best to deal with them. Parents may need some training in helping their children at home, and if their child reaches Stage 4 they should have careful briefing about what is involved in statutory assessment as well as their rights and opportunities.

Wolfendale and Bryans (1978) suggest that the in-service programme should contain the following:

- recapitulation of principles and processes of child development and the psychology of individual differences
- origins and aetiology of behaviour and learning problems
- assessment of learning difficulties in specific areas: language aspects of reading failure, perceptual motor skills
- forms of educational intervention and their organisation
- administration and interpretation of screening results
- opportunities to design, carry out and evaluate under supervision a short intervention programme on individual children or within a small group.

(Wolfendale and Bryans 1978: 249)

THE SKILLS AND KNOWLEDGE NEEDED BY CLASSROOM TEACHERS

Children with special needs require an appropriate programme for the whole day. They should not be merely 'occupied' while others do work which they find too difficult. Nor should class teachers feel that the progress of such children is another's responsibility. All teachers need knowledge of how to enable children with special needs to learn. The grid which is set out in Figure 11.1 provides an opportunity for a school to analyse the practical needs of its teachers by asking each of them to complete a copy. It does not specifically include the kind of background information which the above list by Wolfendale and Bryans suggests, but much of this can be dealt with as part of studying the practical knowledge and skills which teachers need. When completed for each member of staff, the grid will provide the information needed for planning an in-service programme.

Identifying learning problems

It is comparatively easy to recognise the child whose skills are poor, but more difficult to spot children whose work is below their ability. The classroom teacher also needs to be able to recognise signs of poor sight and poor hearing and other physical problems.

Identifying gifted children

Some gifted children will stand out from the beginning of their time in school. Others may have gifts, such as musical ability or athletic skill, which will not be immediately evident and will reveal themselves only

STAFF DEVELOPMENT QUESTIONNAIRE			
Please tick the column which represents your degree of confidence in each of the following areas	Conf-ident	Av.	Not conf-ident
Identifying learning problems			
Identifying gifted children			
Diagnosing the nature of learning problems			
Differentiating work for all abilities			
Knowledge of methods and materials for SEN			
Helping children with reading problems			
Helping children with writing problems			
Helping children with spelling problems			
Helping children with mathematical difficulties			
Dealing with learning problems in other subjects			
Dealing with children with emotional and behavioural problems			
Dealing with children with physical disabilities			
Dealing with children with language problems			
Providing for exceptionally able children			
Managing collaborative group work			
Using information technology for children with special educational needs			
Counselling children			
Working with parents			
Knowledge of support services			
Knowledge of Code of Practice			

Figure 11.1 Staff development questionnaire © Joan Dean 1996

as children have opportunities to study these areas of curriculum. There will also be children who are more able that their contemporaries but have learned to disguise their ability in order to be socially acceptable. Teachers need to be on the alert for such children.

Diagnosing the nature of learning problems

Diagnosis of the nature of learning problems is a continuous process. This should follow on from identifying problems and teachers should be adding to their knowledge of children from their observation all the time they are with them. They need knowledge of what checks to make and how to make and record them when they encounter a child with difficulties. It is in this context that teachers can profitably learn about the causes of some learning problems.

Differentiating work for all abilities

No class is homogeneous and the good teacher plans work so that it takes into account the abilities of all the children. Since all are working to the National Curriculum this may mean finding different routes to the same ends for children with learning difficulties, providing work which can be undertaken at a variety of levels and providing deeper and richer experiences for the exceptionally able.

Knowledge of methods and materials for SEN

Ideally classroom teachers need to be able to draw on a school bank of resources to meet the needs of individuals. They also need to know what they are looking for and have their own materials well organised. This is likely to be most effective when teachers come together to plan their work and to make and find materials which are suitable for children of different abilities. Teachers also need to know how to break down learning into small steps to meet a given objective.

Helping children with reading problems

Teachers of young children should be expert in teaching the beginnings of reading, but may be less confident where the more advanced skills of reading are concerned. Teachers of older children may be confident with the more advanced skills but less certain what to do when they encounter a child who has barely started to read. All primary school teachers need to be expert in all stages of teaching children to read.

Helping children with writing problems

These may be problems of handwriting and/or problems of expression. A child may take an immense amount of time to write very little and the teachers should have ideas about what to do in this case. Such children may produce more if they are allowed to tape what they want to say for someone to type out later. They may also write more if there is a genuine incentive such as the post box described in Chapter 5 (p.86). Teachers also need to know what to do about the child whose handwriting is illegible. This may be because the child has a physical defect. Thus teachers should know something about the defects that are likely to pose problems for children when they come to write. Placing too much emphasis on the problem may make things worse rather than better, but in some cases practising writing patterns may help. It may also be that the child has not been taught how to hold the writing tool and form letters poperly and teaching these may make a difference.

Helping children with spelling problems

Teachers need to know a lot about the English system of spelling, which is more regular than is sometimes supposed. Children vary in the way they learn spelling. Those with serious spelling problems really need to have a thorough knowledge of phonics, and to learn and practise the rules of spelling as well as looking at what different words have in common, using multi-sensory approaches to spelling and saying and writing words. Teachers can learn about the problems children are encountering from studying their errors in spelling; repeated errors of a similar kind show that a child has not grasped a particular spelling rule.

Helping children with mathematical difficulties

Although most teachers in primary schools have a lot of experience in helping children to understand mathematics, the fact remains that many adults confess to a poor understanding even of simple calculations. On the other hand, both adults and children manage to calculate quite well when they have a personal interest in the outcome. In recent years we have become aware of this and school mathematics has contained a good deal more which has relevance to everyday life. Teachers need to discover the way in which children are thinking about mathematical calculations and to look carefully at the errors they are making.

Dealing with learning problems in other subjects

Many of the problems encountered in other subjects are problems concerned with literacy or numeracy. However, this will not be true to any extent of technology, art, music and physical education, and science involves an understanding of the nature of science which some children find difficult to grasp. The problems may be developmental. Some children are held back in their work by physical or cognitive development. In art there may be some children who are still drawing like infant school children at a later age. Problems in technology and science may be helped by collaborative work, provided that children with difficulties do not leave all the work to the others. In art and to some extent music, development may come about through experience, maturity and practice. In physical education a child may be helped by breaking down a movement into small steps which he or she can practise.

Dealing with children with emotional and behavioural problems

Schools need to have agreement among staff about how emotional and behavioural problems should be dealt with. This is probably best summed up in the behaviour policy which can be made clear to children and parents. Chapter 6 on behaviour problems makes a number of suggestions such as behaviour modification and counselling of various kinds.

Dealing with children with physical disabilities

Teachers and other staff will need to know about any children with physical disabilities they have in the school. They also need to know about the nature of the disability and the particular problems it is likely to cause in school. Everyone should know about each child since they may encounter him or her at lunch or in the playground as well as in the classroom. When a new child with a physical disability joins the school there must be an opportunity for everyone to become informed about his or her needs. This category also includes children with hearing or visual impairment and teachers should know about the causes of these problems, what children can be expected to do and the implications for teachers.

Dealing with children with language problems

Language problems may be those of children not speaking English or not speaking standard English, problems in articulation, difficulties over putting words together, stammering and mutism, either elective or as part of a wider disability. Teachers may need to be guided by teachers of English as a foreign language and by speech therapists.

Providing for exceptionally able children

Exceptionally able children are very varied and the teacher must be aware of each child as an individual and provide work which stimulates and challenges. Teachers need to work together to think of ways in which this can be done.

Managing collaborative group work

There is evidence that in many primary classrooms children sit in groups but work as individuals (see Galton *et al.* 1980). Children need the experience of actually working together and helping each other. Ainscow (1994) suggests that 'Cooperative learning is only successful when group activities are planned to encourage positive interdependence between group members' (p.69). This requires good organisation and children need to be taught some of the skills of working together and of leading a group.

Using information technology for children with special educational needs

Information technology has a great deal to offer all children, but is particularly valuable for children with special needs. Teachers must be aware of what it offers and of the software that is available.

Counselling children

Teachers must learn the skills of counselling so that they can deal with children for whom this is needed, particularly those with emotional and behavioural problems, but also children suffering bereavement, family break-up and coming to terms with serious disabilities.

Working with parents

Working with parents requires empathy, skill in negotiation and a readiness to be open-minded. Parents confronted with the fact that their child has special needs may themselves need support and counselling and all teachers should have these skills.

Knowledge of support services

Teachers need to know what services are available to support their work and what each service has to offer.

Knowledge of the Code of Practice

All teachers need to know what the Code of Practice sets out and how their work fits into its ideas.

THE SKILLS AND KNOWLEDGE NEEDED BY COORDINATORS

Teachers in the role of coordinator need all the skills listed above but in greater depth and measure than classroom teachers. They also need a number of other skills and knowledge which are discussed in this section.

Negotiating with and suggesting ideas to adults

The coordinator may need to negotiate for various kinds of additional help for teachers, such as the help which he or she gives in doing some teaching or diagnostic work with children with special needs. Ideas may need to be suggested tactfully, particularly where teachers are experienced but perhaps not skilled at dealing with children with certain kinds of special needs. It may also be necessary to negotiate with the headteacher and the governors over the amounts to be spent on children with special needs. There may be a need to deal tactfully with parents who are concerned about their children and feel that the school is not doing enough for them.

Counselling teachers, parents and children

All teachers need the skills of counselling children, but the coordinator also must be skilled at counselling adults. Teachers may require counselling if they become depressed about the problems they are having with children with special needs, particularly where these concern children with emotional and behavioural difficulties. Parents will often become depressed about their children and may need some counselling about ways of managing the problems they pose. Children too will need counselling by the coordinator as well as by class teachers.

Administrative skills of keeping records

The Code of Practice demands a lot of paperwork. The coordinator must keep records of children registered as having special needs and reviews of their progress. These records will have particular significance if a child reaches the point of having a statutory assessment when all the previous records will be called upon as evidence of what the school has done.

Keeping these records will not just be a matter of storing them but very often it will be a question of seeing that colleagues and parents produce the appropriate statements, and in some cases, particularly with parents, it will be necessary to help them to write the record (this may involve finding someone who speaks the parent's language and who can provide a translated version of what the parent wishes to say).

Managing time

Primary schools are not generously staffed and no coordinator will have time to spare. This makes it important that time is well managed. Coordinators should plan the use of the time they have for special needs work so that everyone gets a fair share. They have to prioritise their work so that important tasks are undertaken in good time. It will also be important to see that time is allocated to managing the paperwork.

Organising the work of others

The coordinator's work may include such tasks as arrangements for the involvement of specialists and the allocation of ancillary and other assistance. It may also involve ensuring that the assistance given in classrooms by both ancillary staff and volunteers is properly organised and that supporters and teachers work as a team. It may be necessary to help class teachers to organise their work so that they have time to give attention to children with special needs.

Teaching colleagues about work with children with special needs

The coordinator has an important staff development role. He or she is the expert in teaching children with special needs and the task is to make everyone else expert. This may mean running courses for colleagues as well as advising from day to day. It may also mean being knowledgeable about books, materials and equipment and advising colleagues on what might be suitable in an individual case.

Knowledge of developments in work with children with special needs

The coordinator must read and study what is happening nationally to develop work with children with special needs and keep in touch with research into this area of work so that colleagues can be kept informed about any development that might be useful to them.

Knowledge of new materials and equipment

The coordinator must keep in touch with what is being published for children with special needs so that the school can use the money it spends on this area of work wisely.

Perhaps the most important characteristics of the good coordinator are the ability to make good relationships easily and depth of knowledge of the area of work.

THE STAFF DEVELOPMENT PROGRAMME

Learning about special needs should feature as part of the staff development programme on a number of occasions. There should also be informal opportunities such as visiting other schools and centres and sharing skills and knowledge. A good coordinator should be prepared to provide some in-service opportunities for colleagues, and the school should be able to draw on the skills of specialists of various kinds according to the topics they wish to discuss at any given time.

When a school is required to integrate a number of children with special needs for the first time, teachers will, not unnaturally, feel apprehensive. They will need an induction programme in the first instance, which gives them a chance to air their concerns and provides information about the problems of the particular children who will be joining them. They may find it helpful to visit the special schools the children will be coming from and to learn about how the teachers there work. They also need the chance to think and talk and plan together so that they draw on all the expertise they have in the school.

For some schools, the Code of Practice will make little difference. They have already most of its provisions in place and their in-service needs will be those of improving the existing knowledge and skills, training newly appointed members of staff where this is required and learning about new problems as children join the school. In other cases there will be a need for intensive in-service work to meet the demands of the Code of Practice. It is suggested that in this case all the teachers complete a copy of the matrix given in Figure 11.1 and that this information is used to plan an in-service programme. This will also show the particular areas in which individual teachers are confident and could perhaps offer help to their colleagues who are less confident. Teachers may also volunteer to read a book on a particular aspect of special needs and talk to their colleagues about it. It may be possible in this way to cover a good deal of ground with the school's own resources. These can be supplemented by inviting teachers who have already experienced integration of children with special needs, teachers from special schools, support teachers, advisers, educational psychologists or other specialists to work with the staff.

In areas where none of the staff is confident, teachers can be sent on courses, with the idea that they can share what they have learned. Mittler, in a foreword to Montgomery (1990), makes the point that: 'There must be a commitment by management to allow the staff member to try to implement ideas and methods learned on the course ' (p.xxiii). It is also important that teachers are supported in their attempts to meet the needs of children. Much in-service work is wasted because it is not followed up in schools. Evaluating the effects of different approaches to provision is very important. Teachers need to reflect on practice and this is often best done in collaboration with colleagues. Children will also have something of value to say about their experience of a particular way of working.

Ainscow (1994) suggests that teachers should negotiate much of what goes on at an in-service course so that it meets their needs. They need to be setting objectives for their own learning supported by the course leaders. They need 'to consider their current ways of working and their existing beliefs and assumptions' (p.40) and perhaps keep journals in which they write about what is happening in their classrooms and their experience of the course. He also stresses the value of group problem-solving and suggests peer coaching involving 'pairs of colleagues working in one another's classrooms to review aspects of their practice and experiment with alternate ways of working' (p.43). He suggests that

> teachers who regard themselves as learners in the classroom are likely to be more successful in facilitating the learning of their pupils. The sensitivity they acquire as a result of reflecting upon their attempts to learn new ideas or new ways of working is influential in terms of the way they deal with children in their classes.
>
> (Ainscow 1994: 190)

There is also a place for more informal approaches to staff development. For example, teachers working on the school policy for special needs or the kind of records they wish to keep learn a great deal in the process. A group or a pair of teachers working together to make materials for the particular needs identified in their classrooms will learn from doing this. Group problem-solving is a good way to learn. Teachers also learn from observation of skilled teaching, perhaps on videotape. They learn particularly from feedback on their own performance, perhaps as part of appraisal, but also specifically in relation to the way they deal with children with special needs. If the coordinator can be freed to observe and provide feedback for colleagues this can be extremely valuable. Similar help might be available occasionally from advisers or advisory teachers.

The special needs coordinator has a large part to play in helping colleagues to learn informally in the context of helping them to deal with particular children. He or she may demonstrate how to deal with some particular problem or show a video or play an audiotape of work with a particular child. Teachers can also role play such activities as dealing with parents who are not very happy about the school telling them that their child has special needs.

Wolfendale (1992b) suggests 'preparing and discussing "case studies" of children in school; using these as exemplars for the evolution of classroom practice, curriculum innovation, how to meet the specific needs of children with sensory or physical disabilities' (p.118). She also suggests a teacher doing an exchange for a short time with a teacher in a special school. Postlethwaite and Hackney (1988) stress the value of asking children what they think, and the Code of Practice requires the involvement of the child in the plans being made for him or her. In particular, children may have ideas about the best way of learning for them.

Discussion about special needs, including the education of the exceptionally able, should be included in many of the courses planned for teachers. All subject area courses dealing with the National Curriculum need to include work on special educational needs.

ISSUES FOR CONSIDERATION

- Are all teachers and other staff aware of the school policy for children with special needs?
- Does the school policy encourage classroom teachers to see children with special needs as their responsibility in the first instance and a challenge to professional skill in problem-solving? Is the headteacher working to support this view?
- What skills and knowledge of special needs teaching has each teacher? Has anyone skills and knowledge which could be used as part of an in-service programme for the rest of the staff?
- Are we using the advent of a child with special needs as an opportunity for the class teacher to develop the skills of observation and to acquire further knowledge?
- When a new teacher joins the staff, do we discuss what that teacher knows about special needs teaching and suggest ways in which he or she can fill any gaps in knowledge?
- Do teachers work with each other to explore the problems of children with special needs?
- Has work with children with special needs played a part in any of the school's in-service days?
- Have any teachers recently attended a course on special needs?
- Does the coordinator see him- or herself as advising classroom teachers, supporting their work and developing their skills?
- What is the role of the peripatetic specialist teacher? Is he or she being used as effectively as possible?
- What opportunities are there locally to help teachers to improve their skill and knowledge?
- Are teachers aware of the need to make provision for exceptionally able children as well as those with learning difficulties? Do they do anything about it?

Chapter 12

Evaluation

The governors, headteacher and staff must assess from time to time the effectiveness of their provision for children with special needs. Primary schools tend to evaluate their work informally rather than making a point of reviewing in a more formal way. The Code of Practice (DFE 1994c) requires that: 'The annual report for each school shall include a report containing such information as may be prescribed about the implementation of the governing body's policy for pupils with special educational needs' (para. 2.10, p.9). The governing body's report must include information on:

- the success of the SEN policy
- significant changes in the policy
- any consultation with the LEA, the Funding Authority and other schools
- how resources have been allocated to and amongst children with special educational needs over the year.

(DFE 1994c: paras 2.10 and 2.11, p.9)

This suggests that a more formal review of what has happened over the course of the year is needed. The staff need to know how effective they have been

- with individual children with special educational needs
- in organising for special educational needs;
- in developing the work of teachers and adding to their knowledge of special educational needs.

At the very least these areas need to be evaluated as part of the preparation for the annual parents' meeting in order to be able to make a statement about the success of the special needs policy.

In addition the school must review the work of all children with statements. This requires the headteacher to convene a meeting to assist in preparing for review, and which includes the parents and relevant staff members, anyone suggested by the LEA and anyone else the headteacher considers appropriate. Copies of all the information received must be circulated before the meeting, and the head must then submit the review report to the LEA by the specified date.

Before the meeting and in preparation for review, the headteacher must seek written advice from the parents, from the class teacher, from anyone suggested by the LEA and anyone else considered appropriate. This should be concerned with the progress the child has made towards meeting the objectives in the statement and meeting any targets agreed. It should also be concerned with the progress the child has made in the National Curriculum, and the continued appropriateness of the statement, including any transition plan or amendments to the statement. There should also be a consideration of whether the statement should continue to be maintained. There will also be a case for evaluating materials and approaches.

METHODS OF EVALUATION

There are a number of different ways of evaluating what is happening.

Observation, interviewing and discussion

All teachers evaluate by observing. Children react to what the teacher says and does and the teacher reacts to their responses. Teachers look at the work of children and draw conclusions about how well they have or have not learned. The accuracy of these judgements depends upon the experience, knowledge and sensitivity of the teacher. The judgements can be made more valid if more than one person observes the same situation. Judgements about children's work are more accurate if the teacher discusses it with someone else. The coordinator for special needs should be able to provide a second opinion which is knowledgeable and informed and the school should discuss and evaluate the work of all the children on the special needs register on a regular basis. Children's records will provide a basis for this discussion, giving information about how well they are progressing and their areas of difficulty. There ought to be regular discussions with children and their parents about the progress of the Individual Education Plans.

A skilled and experienced observer can take into account many things which are important but which would not be easy to measure. For example, it is important that children with special needs develop confidence, self-esteem and independence and a teacher can assess this from the way children react and behave and from talking with them. Even with the more measurable aspects of work, observation can cover more ground and place learning in context more easily than testing. The opinions of a skilled and experienced teacher are known to be pretty reliable.

A view of the progress of individual children will also be gained by interviewing parents and children about how much progress they feel is being made and how happy they are with the way the problems are being handled. This might be part of the discussion evaluating the progress of children or it might be done separately.

The staff should also discuss how they feel the organisation for special needs is working. Are the arrangements adequate for identifying the children who have special needs, assessing those needs and diagnosing problems? Is the recording system satisfactory and is it working? Is the involvement of parents working well? Is there coordination of work and continuity for the children throughout the school? Is enough provision being made for children who are exceptionally able? Is time being used to the best effect? Are the resources adequate and available? Are they being used? Could more use be made of computers or other audiovisual materials? Could greater use be made of parents and other visitors? Is enough use being made of the support services? Is the organisation the best possible with the resources available? Are there links with other schools to maintain continuity for children with special needs?

There should also be discussion and perhaps interviewing of individual teachers about their development needs in relation to special needs. In what areas do they feel they need more knowledge or skill? What would they like to see about special needs in the staff development programme? Is the school using sufficiently the skills that some teachers possess? Does the way that special needs work is organised do anything to increase the skills of classroom teachers? What do people feel they have learned since last year? The lists of questions in the issues for consideration sections at the end of the chapters in this book may also provide useful material for discussion.

If teachers or parents or children are interviewed the interviewer needs to decide whether to ask everyone the same questions or whether simply to follow up answers to an initial question. When you ask everyone the same questions you have information which you can compare. You also get an overall picture of how everyone is seeing things. When you let the interview go where it will you often get information which is interesting and valuable but may be particular to the individual.

Questionnaires

It is helpful at some stage in evaluation to use questionnaires. These can be of various types. A questionnaire can ask open-ended questions so that people can give opinions. Alternatively it can pose questions which ask for a rating of how well people think something has gone – how good is the organisation of special needs, for example.

In using questionnaires one should avoid questions which are in any way ambiguous or which combine more than one question. It is important not to make the questionnaire too long – one page is the length to aim for. If it is too long people will not complete it. It also needs to be clearly laid out with enough space for the kind of answers that are wanted. The space left for answers gives those completing the questionnaire clues about how much is expected.

It can be helpful to use questionnaires and then to follow them up with interviews or discussions about the outcome. The advantage of using questionnaires is that they produce a reaction from everyone who replies that is not influenced by what other people think, which may be the case in discussion.

Testing

Judgements made by observation need to be checked occasionally by testing. Tests might be regarded as a step towards making evaluation more objective. All teachers devise tests for their own use and there is a place for using standardised tests from time to time with children with special needs. In addition there will be the results of the SATs (Standard Attainment Tests) for children in the appropriate age groups. Tests should be selected or compiled according to the purpose for which they are needed.

Testing may be to discover:

* whether a child is ready for the next stage of work – testing here might be to discover what the child knows and can do in a limited area of work;
* whether the child has acquired the skill, knowledge or understanding required by a piece of work;
* how the child performs relative to his or her peer group;
* how to group children for learning;
* the effectiveness of particular materials or organisation for learning and teaching.

Standardised tests need to be carefully selected to supplement teacher-devised tests and a list of tests available to teachers in numeracy and literacy is given in Appendix 2. In selecting a test the following points need to be borne in mind:

* Does this test meet the purposes we have in mind?
  Tests are devised with particular purposes and a test which is devised to identify less able children will not be equally good at identifying the very able. Some tests also cover very little ground. A word recognition test, for example, tells you very little about the child's ability

to deal with continuous text with understanding or about learning problems. When the time required for testing individuals is taken into account, word recognition tests do not appear to be very good value. It is wise also to look at the date a test was standardised. If this is a long time ago the test may be somewhat suspect.

- Is it appropriate for the age group we wish to test?
  Test catalogues normally give the age group for which the test was devised.
- What is involved in administering it?
  It is necessary to take into account the arrangements which will be needed for children to take the test and the teacher time involved in giving it and marking it.
- Can we afford it?
  Tests cost a good deal of money and this must be weighed up against the value of the information likely to come from using them.

Check-lists

Check-lists might be regarded as another form of testing. They are particularly useful in assessing what a child does and does not know and providing guidance for the teacher as to what needs to be done. They also provide a useful record. Some check-lists of phonic skills are given in Appendix 1.

Points to note about evaluation

- It is important to sample carefully.
  The evidence which a teacher uses in assessing what a child knows and can do, or the effectiveness of particular materials or approaches, or the evidence a coordinator might use in assessing how successful a course for teachers has been, is only a sample of what the child can do or the effectiveness of the approach. It is necessary to consider whether the sample is representative.
- Assessments need to be valid and reliable.
  A piece of evidence or a test score is said to be valid if it actually reflects what it sets out to reflect. This is normally determined by correlating the result with some other evidence. Thus a teacher's judgement about a child's performance is likely to be more valid if another teacher comes to the same conclusion or if test scores confirm the teacher's opinion.
    Evidence is reliable if it is likely that the answers will be similar if the same item is checked again. Thus a test of arithmetic given to particular pupils on one occasion is likely to be a reliable test of their knowledge of the arithmetic tested if those pupils achieve similar

scores given the same, or an alternative version of the same test on another occasion (assuming that they have not received further teaching between the two tests).

• Assessment can be formative or summative.

Formative assessment is assessment made while something is happening so that the assessment helps to form the outcome. Summative assessment is assessment made when the work is completed.

• Assessment involves looking from different viewpoints.

It is easy to see something from too limited a point of view. A teacher may feel that the work is going well but the child and the parents may see it differently. It is important in evaluating work to seek deliberately to get views from different people, particularly parents and children.

• Subjectivity and objectivity need to be balanced.

Subjective judgement has the advantage that it can be faster and can take in more aspects of the work than objective tests. It can be made more objective by combining the observations of different people or by comparing it with test results. It is also valuable to use standardised tests from time to time, but it should be remembered that their outcome is not necessarily more accurate than the judgement of an experienced teacher who may be taking more evidence into account.

THE EVALUATION TASKS OF THE COORDINATOR

The coordinator of special educational needs has overall responsibility for evaluation, and the tasks involved in this were listed in Chapter 4. The coordinator is the leader for the evaluation tasks involved. Undertaking these tasks involves the activities listed below:

Ensuring that class teachers identify children who may have special needs

This involves seeing that class teachers are aware of the observations and checks they need to make, that they are aware of the details of the registration forms they are to complete, that they know that identifying a child means discussing the issues with the parents, and that they are aware of the arrangements for doing this and for evaluating the success of these activities.

Monitoring the progress of children identified as having special needs

The coordinator has an overall responsibility for all the children registered as having special needs. This involves checking with class teachers how these children are doing from time to time and working with the class teacher to evaluate their progress against the Individual Education Plans.

Leading the staff evaluation of the effectiveness of the overall organisation

The coordinator should be the main person setting up the evaluation process in the school, conducting and leading the discussions and interviews, and producing the questionnaires and tests.

Leading the staff in evaluating the effectiveness of staff development

The coordinator also needs to set up the evaluation process for staff development, but since he or she may have been instrumental in providing some of the staff training, this may be a matter of asking someone else to set up the evaluation and discuss with staff how they found the arrangements made for some of the evaluation. The coordinator may lead other parts of the evaluation, such as evaluation of the courses members of staff have attended or activities run by other people.

Considering whether the school is achieving the aims of the policy

There is an overall need to consider whether the intentions of the policy are being met. This will be a matter of considering the outcomes of the other areas which are being evaluated.

JUDGING THE EFFECTIVENESS OF EVALUATION

Evaluation needs to be followed by a consideration of its effectiveness:

- Was it worth the time spent?
- Would a different way of working have been better?
- Is there anything that can be learned from the way the evaluation was carried out which could be applied on another occasion?
- Could more be done to collect assessment information as part of everyday work?

Many schools do a useful job in evaluating the progress of individual children with special needs but do little about evaluating wider issues such as the effectiveness of the organisation or the arrangements for staff development. Unless wider issues are evaluated regularly it is unlikely that the highest possible standards will be reached. Important problems will attract attention and may be solved, but, rather as the quiet child in the class is sometimes missed, so aspects of work which could be more effective remain unexamined and may be missed.

It is also important to remember that evaluation takes time and needs to be planned into the work schedule. If there is good planning, much evidence for evaluation can be collected as work proceeds and simply gathered together at the end of the year.

ISSUES FOR CONSIDERATION

- How shall we evaluate the success of the special needs policy?
- How shall we evaluate the effectiveness of the special needs organisation?
- How shall we evaluate the effectiveness of the staff development programme for special needs?
- What use shall we make of observation in our evaluation programme?
- What use shall we make of interviewing and what questions shall we ask?
- Whom shall we question?
- What use shall we make of questionnaires and what questions shall we ask?
- Whom shall we ask to complete the questionnaires?
- What use shall we make of testing and check-lists?
- How shall we ensure that our evidence is valid and reliable?
- Who will be involved in each part of our evaluation?
- How shall we assess the effectiveness of our evaluation?

Chapter 13

Conclusion

Teachers in primary schools are well used to making provision for children with a wide range of needs and abilities. Making provision for children with special needs, those with learning problems, those with emotional and behavioural problems, those with physical problems and those who are exceptionally able is an extension of this and requires the same sorts of skill, although in some cases a child will need special work in nearly all aspects of curriculum and this can pose considerable problems for the individual teacher. It helps if teachers work together to produce material for children with serious difficulties.

As developments proceed there should also be considerable help from new technology. In theory, computers can identify a child's problems and match them with appropriate work. In practice this ability has not yet been developed to any extent. We are nevertheless moving to a situation where a great deal can be done with computers and where within the foreseeable future there will be many schools where every child has a laptop and uses this for a good deal of work. In particular, computers offer the possibility of drafting writing and then improving it so that everyone produces good looking work The use of concept keyboards and overlays of various kinds can also provide opportunities for children who have learning problems. Computers can present material in a variety of ways so that children who need much repetition can be provided with it. Teachers need to keep a careful watch on what is being published so that they can take advantage of appropriate software.

This is not to suggest that computers replace teachers. What they may be able to do is to free teachers for the things that only a person can do. Only the teacher can work with children in groups, helping them to learn from each other through discussion. Except in fairly simple situations where something is right or wrong, only the teacher can help a child evaluate the work he or she has done. Only the teacher can help with planning work. Only the teacher can decide what can appropriately be done with computers and what needs a different approach.

Only the teacher can see the relationships between different parts of the curriculum and link them in children's minds, and develop such activities as drama and group art work and music-making, although both art and music can benefit from the use of a computer.

The teacher is the most important source of stimulus and inspiration for children. No technology can replace the effect of the enthusiastic teacher who is able to pass this enthusiasm on to children. Such teachers often perform miracles in getting children to learn and it is perhaps because of such teachers that we are aware of the tremendous power to learn in most children if only we can find a way of tapping it.

Almost every child achieves the tremendous intellectual task of learning to speak before he or she comes to school. The child learns this, not by being taught in a formal sense, but by working it out from what is happening and from the speech in his or her home environment. A person who can achieve so much at such a young age surely has more potential than we have yet been able to develop in schools. This should give us hope for all children whatever their problems.

Appendix 1
Check-lists

The alphabet

Knows letter names – lower case

	a	b	c	d	e	f	g	h	i	j	k	l	m
Says	☐	☐	☐	☐	☐	☐	☐	☐	☐	☐	☐	☐	☐
Writes	☐	☐	☐	☐	☐	☐	☐	☐	☐	☐	☐	☐	☐

	n	o	p	q	r	s	t	u	v	w	x	y	z
Says	☐	☐	☐	☐	☐	☐	☐	☐	☐	☐	☐	☐	☐
Writes	☐	☐	☐	☐	☐	☐	☐	☐	☐	☐	☐	☐	☐

Knows letter sounds – lower case

	a	b	c	d	e	f	g	h	i	j	k	l	m
Says	☐	☐	☐	☐	☐	☐	☐	☐	☐	☐	☐	☐	☐
Writes	☐	☐	☐	☐	☐	☐	☐	☐	☐	☐	☐	☐	☐

	n	o	p	q	r	s	t	u	v	w	x	y	z
Says	☐	☐	☐	☐	☐	☐	☐	☐	☐	☐	☐	☐	☐
Writes	☐	☐	☐	☐	☐	☐	☐	☐	☐	☐	☐	☐	☐

Notes of child's performance:

continued/...

Knows letter names – upper case

	A	B	C	D	E	F	G	H	I	J	K	L	M
Says	☐	☐	☐	☐	☐	☐	☐	☐	☐	☐	☐	☐	☐
Writes	☐	☐	☐	☐	☐	☐	☐	☐	☐	☐	☐	☐	☐

	N	O	P	Q	R	S	T	U	V	W	X	Y	Z
Says	☐	☐	☐	☐	☐	☐	☐	☐	☐	☐	☐	☐	☐
Writes	☐	☐	☐	☐	☐	☐	☐	☐	☐	☐	☐	☐	☐

Knows letter sounds – upper case

	A	B	C	D	E	F	G	H	I	J	K	L	M
Says	☐	☐	☐	☐	☐	☐	☐	☐	☐	☐	☐	☐	☐
Writes	☐	☐	☐	☐	☐	☐	☐	☐	☐	☐	☐	☐	☐

	N	O	P	Q	R	S	T	U	V	W	X	Y	Z
Says	☐	☐	☐	☐	☐	☐	☐	☐	☐	☐	☐	☐	☐
Writes	☐	☐	☐	☐	☐	☐	☐	☐	☐	☐	☐	☐	☐

Notes of child's performance:

CHECK-LIST 2

Recognition of single sounds in words

Reads	bib ☐	cut ☐	dim ☐	fed ☐
Writes	☐	☐	☐	☐
Reads	got ☐	hut ☐	job ☐	kit ☐
Writes	☐	☐	☐	☐
Reads	lap ☐	mat ☐	nod ☐	pat ☐
Writes	☐	☐	☐	☐
Reads	rip ☐	sat ☐	tip ☐	vet ☐
Writes	☐	☐	☐	☐
Reads	win ☐	mix ☐	yet ☐	zip ☐
Writes	☐	☐	☐	☐

Notes of child's performance:

CHECK-LIST 3

Recognition of two letter initial blends in words

Reads	blot ☐	clap ☐	flap ☐	glad ☐
Writes	☐	☐	☐	☐
Reads	plan ☐	slot ☐	bran ☐	crab ☐
Writes	☐	☐	☐	☐
Reads	drop ☐	frill ☐	grab ☐	pram ☐
Writes	☐	☐	☐	☐
Reads	trot ☐	scab ☐	skip ☐	smut ☐
Writes	☐	☐	☐	☐
Reads	snap ☐	spot ☐	stop ☐	swim ☐
Writes	☐	☐	☐	☐
Reads	swan ☐	twin ☐		
Writes	☐	☐		

Notes of child's performance:

CHECK-LIST 4

Recognition of two letter ending blends in words

Reads	du<u>ck</u> ☐	fa<u>ct</u> ☐	le<u>ft</u> ☐	la<u>mp</u> ☐
Writes	☐	☐	☐	☐
Reads	be<u>nd</u> ☐	ri<u>ng</u> ☐	se<u>nt</u> ☐	ha<u>lf</u> ☐
Writes	☐	☐	☐	☐
Reads	ta<u>lk</u> ☐	bo<u>lt</u> ☐	ne<u>st</u> ☐	we<u>pt</u> ☐
Writes	☐	☐	☐	☐
Reads	bu<u>lb</u> ☐	to<u>ld</u> ☐	fi<u>lm</u> ☐	si<u>nk</u> ☐
Writes	☐	☐	☐	☐
Reads	ma<u>sk</u> ☐			
Writes	☐			

Notes of child's performance:

© Joan Dean 1996

CHECK-LIST 5

Recognition of three letter initial blends in words

Reads	s<u>cr</u>ub ☐	s<u>pl</u>it ☐	s<u>tr</u>ing ☐	s<u>hr</u>ink ☐
Writes	☐	☐	☐	☐

Reads	s<u>pr</u>ing ☐	<u>thr</u>ee ☐	s<u>qu</u>ib ☐
Writes	☐	☐	☐

Recognition of three letter ending blends in words

Reads	wa<u>tch</u> ☐	ba<u>dge</u> ☐
Writes	☐	☐

Recognition of two letter digraphs in words

Reads	mu<u>ch</u> ☐	ba<u>ck</u> ☐	fi<u>sh</u> ☐	tee<u>th</u> ☐
Writes	☐	☐	☐	☐

Reads	<u>ch</u>ip ☐	<u>th</u>en ☐	<u>sh</u>op ☐	<u>th</u>in ☐
Writes	☐	☐	☐	☐

Notes of child's performance:

Recognition of long vowel sounds with marker 'e'

Reads	l<u>a</u>ne ☐	m<u>i</u>ne ☐	h<u>o</u>me ☐	t<u>u</u>ne ☐
Writes	☐	☐	☐	☐

Recognition of other spellings of long vowel sounds

Reads	t<u>ai</u>l ☐	pl<u>ay</u> ☐	b<u>ee</u>n ☐	r<u>ea</u>d ☐
Writes	☐	☐	☐	☐

Reads	tr<u>y</u> ☐	n<u>igh</u>t ☐	b<u>oa</u>t ☐	sh<u>ow</u> ☐
Writes	☐	☐	☐	☐

Reads	f<u>ew</u> ☐	tr<u>ue</u> ☐	b<u>oo</u>t ☐
Writes	☐	☐	☐

Notes of child's performance:

Appendix 2
Tests available to teachers

Based on a list compiled by the Surrey School Psychological Service

EARLY YEARS TESTS

Early years, easy screen

Authors   J. Clerehugh, K. Hart, K. Rider, K. Turner
Publisher   NFER-Nelson
Age range   4 years–5 years
Time needed   Untimed

Outline   A structured guide to help the teacher determine
              children's development during their first six months
              at school. It identifies different strengths and needs,
              enables the teacher to develop individual teaching
              plans and offers detailed follow-up activities.
                  It covers six skill areas:

              • pencil coordination skills;
              • active body skills;
              • number skills;
              • oral language skills;
              • visual reading skills;
              • auditory reading skills.

Early Maths Diagnostic Kit

Authors   David and Margaret Lumb
Publisher   NFER-Nelson
Age range   4 years–8 years and older children with learning
              difficulties
Time needed   Untimed

| Outline | This covers the main areas of early mathematics work and reflects everyday activities in a typical infant classroom. The handbook suggests follow-up activities that will help the child to overcome areas of difficulty identified. |

LARR test of emergent literacy

Authors	Based on the original test by John Downing, Brian Schafer and J. Douglas Ayres
Publisher	NFER-Nelson
Age range	4 years–5 years 3 months
Time needed	Untimed, but takes about 25 minutes

| Outline | Identifies the extent of each child's development on entering school. Can be administered to groups of up to four children at one time. Focuses on three areas of early reading skills: |

- recognising readable material in various forms;
- identifying when reading and writing are taking place;
- understanding of the basic technical terms of reading in English.

GROUP READING TESTS

London Reading Test

Authors	Centre for Educational Research LSE and NFER
Publisher	NFER-Nelson
Age range	10 years 7 months–12 years 14 months
Time needed	Untimed

| Outline | This is a comprehension test specifically designed for assessing the reading ability of children at the transfer stage. It is particularly suitable for identifying lower ability pupils who may need further support with their reading. Each test consists of three comprehension passages, the first two using cloze procedure. The final passage is followed by a series of questions covering a range of skills. The most recently published forms of the test are particularly suitable for schools with a multi-ethnic population. |

NFER-Nelson Group Reading Test 6–12

Authors	The Macmillan Test Unit
Publisher	NFER-Nelson
Age range	6 years 3 months–13 years 3 months
Time needed	Untimed, approximately 30 minutes

Outline	This is a multiple-choice sentence-completion test designed for whole class use. There are two parallel forms which enable the teacher to monitor progress. It is suitable for screening children with special needs on entry to junior school.

NFER-Nelson Group Reading Test 9–14

Authors	The Macmillan Test Unit
Publisher	NFER-Nelson
Age range	8 years 3 months–15 years 3 months
Time needed	Untimed, approximately 30 minutes

Outline	This test places more emphasis on the comprehension of sentences and passages by asking children to identify missing words within the body of the text. There are two parallel forms which enable the teacher to monitor progress.

Spar Reading Test (second edition)

Author	D. Young
Publisher	Hodder and Stoughton
Age range	6 years–13 years
Time needed	13 minutes

Outline	The Spar Reading test is intended to assess the development of reading and spelling skills among children of a wide range of ability from 7 to 8 year olds to less able secondary pupils. These tests have the greatest reliability and validity in the lower age range.

Suffolk Reading Scale

Author	Fred Hagley
Publisher	NFER-Nelson
Age range	6 years 4 months–13 years 11 months
Time needed	Untimed, approximately 20 minutes

Outline   This is a test of multiple-choice sentence-completion
                items. It is arranged in three levels:

                • Level 1 – age 6+ and 7+ years
                • Level 2 – age 8+, 9+ and 10+ years
                • Level 3 – age 10+, 11+ and 12+ years

                It should help teachers to choose suitable reading
                materials for individuals by gauging what each child
                is able to read as well as evaluating the standard of
                reading.

Widespan Reading test

Authors   Alan Brimer and Herbert Gross
Publisher   NFER-Nelson
Age Range   7 years–14 years
Time needed   30 minutes

Outline   A sentence reading test with a high comprehension
                element. Widespan attempts to assess a child's ability
                to use context and syntax to make correct predictions
                in reading. There are two parallel forms of the test
                enabling teachers to monitor progress.

Young Reading Test (third edition)

Author   D. Young
Publisher   Hodder and Stoughton
Age range   6 years 4 months–11 years 11 months
Time needed   13 minutes

Outline   This test gives a reliable picture of a child's use of
                picture, context, sight and phonic cues and an overall
                measure of independence, accuracy and understanding
                in silent reading. The test can be used with a full class
                with one teacher.

INDIVIDUAL READING TESTS

Edwards' Reading Test

Authors   Peter Edwards and Ruth Nichols
Publisher   Heinemann
Age range   6 years–13 years
Time needed   Untimed

Outline	The test contains both word recognition and prose reading tasks. The authors have attempted to help the teacher decide on appropriate reading books based on a child's reading accuracy, comprehension and recall. The test is based on work related to readability measurement and informal reading inventories.

Neale Analysis of Reading Ability

Author	M.D. Neale; British adaptation: Una Christophers and Chris Whetton
Publisher	NFER-Nelson
Age range	5 years–13 years
Time needed	Untimed, approximately 20 minutes

Outline	This test contains three parallel forms. Each test consists of six short passages of increasing length and complexity. Information is provided about a child's reading accuracy, comprehension and speed of reading. There are also several diagnostic tests to be used selectively with children. On the record sheet the teacher is encouraged to indicate the types of error made by the pupil, i.e., mispronunciations, substitutions, omissions and reversals.
This test should help the teacher to match reading materials to children's abilities, diagnose individual needs in order to take appropriate action and check that specific skills have been acquired.

Salford's Sentence Reading Test

Author	G.E. Bookbinder
Publisher	Hodder and Stoughton
Age range	6 years–10 years 6 months
Time needed	Untimed, approximately 5 minutes

Outline	The test consists of thirteen sentences of increasing order of difficulty. There are parallel forms of it.

TESTS OF REASONING ABILITY

Cognitive Abilities Test

Authors	Robert L. Thorndike, Elisabeth Hagen and Norman France

Publisher   NFER-Nelson
Age range   7 years 6 months–15 years 9 months
Time needed   20 minutes for the practice test, 30 minutes for each
                ability area

Outline   This test measures ability in three main areas:

- Verbal – vocabulary, sentence completion, verbal
  classification and verbal analogies; emphasises
  ability to reason with words and word structure
  and to use words in context.
- Quantitative – quantitative relations, number series
  and equation building; assesses the ability to reason
  with numbers and symbols, which is linked to
  potential for achievement in science and mathematics.
- Non-verbal – figure classification, figure analysis
  and figure synthesis; measures the ability to reason
  with geometric or spatial elements without verbal
  influences.

This test gives teachers the opportunity to assess
ability in comparison with attainment.

NFER-Nelson Verbal Reasoning Test Series

Authors   NFER
Publisher   NFER-Nelson
Age range   7 years 3 months–14 years 3 months
Time needed   Varies

Outline   This test was standardised in 1992 and is intended to
                help teachers to:

- calculate the extent to which the school has
  encouraged the children to achieve their
  potential by making it possible to compare
  children's ability with their performance in
  attainment tests;
- identify those children who may be
  underachieving;
- assess children's potential in an objective way;
- organise effective combinations of children for
  group work.

NFER-Nelson Non-Verbal Reasoning Test Series

Authors	NFER
Publisher	NFER-Nelson
Age range	7 years 3 months–15 years 3 months
Time needed	Varies

Outline   This test has similar purposes to those of the verbal reasoning test above.

INDIVIDUAL TESTS OF ABILITY

British Picture Vocabulary Scales

Authors	Lloyd M. Dunn, Leona M. Dunn, Chris Whetton, David Pintilie
Publisher	NFER-Nelson
Age range	2 years 6 months–18 years
Time needed	Untimed, approximately 20 minutes for the long form and 10 minutes for the short form

Outline   The pupil has to identify which of graded sets of four pictures represents a word spoken by the teacher. This is a very quick and simple test to administer which provides a rough estimate of a child's receptive vocabulary.

Raven's Progressive Matrices and Vocabulary Scales

Author	J.C. Raven
Publisher	NFER-Nelson
Age range	5 years–adult
Time	Untimed; approximately 20 minutes per scale

Outline   There are three levels of tests and the teacher chooses the one which is most suitable for the children concerned. The individual is presented with a series of logically arranged coloured patterns and has to choose which of six alternative pieces to fit into a missing section. The vocabulary test requires the individual to define a graded series of words. These are useful tests, easy to administer, which can provide a quick estimate of a person's vocabulary and perceptual reasoning ability. Scores are given as percentiles.

TESTS OF OTHER SKILLS

Diagnostic and Remedial Spelling Manual

Author	Margaret Peters
Publisher	Macmillan Education
Age range	8 years–11 years
Time needed	Untimed, approximately 40 minutes

Outline   This test helps the teacher to analyse a child's spelling errors. It contains three graded dictation passages, a method of error analysis and guidelines for remedial activity.

The test and manual provide the teacher with a wealth of help and advice for a child with spelling problems.

Mathematics Attainment Test series

Author	NFER	
Publisher	NFER-Nelson	
Age range	Test A	7 years–8 years 6 months
	Test B	8 years–10 years 6 months
	Test C	9 years–12 years
	Test DE2	10 years–11 years 11 months
Time needed	Untimed; approximately 45–50 minutes	

Outline   The tests consist of printed material, some of which is pictorial and diagrammatic. Emphasis is placed on understanding the operations rather than on mechanical procedures. Tests A and B are administered orally. The rest require written answers.

Nottingham Number Test

Authors	W.E.C. Gillingham and K.A. Hesse
Publisher	University of London Press
Age range	9 years 1 month–11 years
Time needed	Untimed, approximately 50–55 minutes

Outline   The test consists of printed questions with some diagrammatic and pictorial material assessing both concepts and calculation skills. Children provide written answers. The scoring enables the teacher to obtain separate mathematics quotients for concepts and calculation skills which may help to determine future teaching goals.

Richmond Test of Basic Skills

Authors	A.N. Heironymous, E.F. Lindquist and N. France
Publisher	NFER-Nelson
Age range	8 years–14 years
Time needed	Varies according to tests used, 5 hours needed for all tests

Outline	This test originated in America and has been adapted and standardised for pupils in Britain. The tests cover the following areas:

1 vocabulary;
2 reading comprehension;
3 language skills;
4 work study skills;
5 mathematics skills.

The Richmond Test of Basic Skills is used regularly in many schools to monitor children's progress.

DIAGNOSTIC TESTS

A number of diagnostic tests are now available to teachers for the analysis of children's learning difficulties. The use of these should enable a teacher to make more effective provision.

Aston Index

Authors	M.J. Newton and M.E. Thompson
Publisher	LDA
Age range	5 years–14 years
Time needed	Untimed, approximately 45 minutes

Outline	This material consists of a test battery developed by the Language Development Research Unit at Aston University. It can be used at two levels.

• Level 1 – as a screening device to identify young children who are likely to experience significant learning difficulties.

- Level 2 – as an analytical device to assess the nature and extent of a child's learning difficulty once it becomes apparent.

The test battery contains items which attempt to provide information in the following areas:

1 attainment in literacy skills;
2 general ability;
3 auditory and visual perceptual skills;
4 graphmotor skills.

A profile of the child's abilities is thus obtained which forms the basis for remedial intervention.

This test battery is time-consuming but provides valuable information to teachers confronted with a child with complex learning difficulties who is not responding to teaching.

Aston Portfolio

Authors	Carol Aubrey, Jane Eaves, Carolyn Hicks and Margaret Newton
Publisher	LDA
Age range	Non-specified
Time needed	Untimed

Outline	The Aston Portfolio is a resource box to help teachers to assess and develop remedial programmes for children with learning difficulties. It can be used independently or with the Aston Index. Advice and teaching suggestions are given in the following areas:

1 reading;
2 spelling;
3 handwriting;
4 comprehension;
5 written expression.

This is a useful source of ideas and practical suggestions to help the class teacher organise remedial work for children. It does not attempt to programme the teacher to respond in a uniform way to a problem but provides a wealth of ideas that can be translated by the teacher into teaching activities. It is a useful source of advice and ideas for a classroom teacher trying to adapt teaching to children with learning problems.

The Barking Reading Project

Author	Barking and Dagenham School Psychological Service
Publisher	London Borough of Barking School Psychological Service
Age range	6 years–11 years
Time needed	45 minutes

Outline   The Barking Project material helps the teacher to make a comprehensive assessment of a child's difficulties. The information provided forms the basis for remedial action. The assessment examines a number of reading-related skills to produce a profile of a child's strengths and weaknesses. An individual remedial programme can then be devised from the extensive range of worksheets and activities provided. The teacher is advised to teach through a child's strengths while simultaneously tackling areas of particular difficulty through remedial work.

Middle Infant Screening Test and Forward Together Programme

Authors	Sybil Hannavy
Publisher	NFER-Nelson
Age range	Around 6 years
Time needed	Untimed, takes approximately 60 minutes

Outline   This material provides a comprehensive screening, diagnostic and follow-up package for children in their fifth and sixth term in school. It enables the teacher to:

- test children's listening and literacy skills;
- obtain a profile of class performance;
- identify the lowest 20 to 25 per cent of children in reading and writing;
- obtain diagnostic information on which to base a follow-up programme.

Quest

Authors	Alistair H. Robertson, Anne Henderson, Ann Robertson, Joanna Fisher and Mike Gibson

Publisher   NFER-Nelson
Age range   7 years–8 years
Time needed   Untimed, takes approximately 30 minutes

Outline   This test provides help and support in identifying
               children who are having difficulties with word
               identification skills, reading comprehension and
               basic number concepts. It also provides materials for
               individual diagnosis and follow-up activities.

References

Ainscow, M. (1994) *Special Needs in the Classroom: A Teacher Education Guide*, France: UNESCO and London: Jessica Kingsley Publishers Ltd.

Ainscow, M. and Muncey, J. (1989) *Meeting Individual Needs in the Primary School*, London: David Fulton.

Ainscow, M. and Tweddle, D.A. (1983) *Preventing Classroom Failure*, London: David Fulton.

—— (1988) *Encouraging Classroom Success*, London: David Fulton.

Audit Commission (1994) *Seen but not Heard*, London: HMSO.

Bennett, N., Desforges, C., Cockburn, A. and Wilkinson, B. (1984) *The Quality of Pupil Learning Experiences*, London: Lawrence Erlbaum Associates.

Bentley, A., Russell, P. and Stobbs, P. (1994) *An Agenda for Action*, London: National Children's Bureau.

Bines, H. (1992) 'Developing roles in the new era', *Support for Learning*, Vol. 7, No. 2, May: 58–62.

Brown, B. (1992) 'Providing for special educational needs within the primary curriculum', in Jones, K. and Charlton, T. (eds), *Learning Difficulties in Primary Classrooms: Delivering the Whole Curriculum*, London: Routledge.

Callow, R. (1994) 'Classroom provision for the able and exceptionally able', *Support for Learning*, Vol. 9, No. 4, November: 151–4.

Chaikin, A.E., Sigler, A. and Derlaga, U. (1974) 'Non-verbal mediators of teacher expectancy effect', *Journal of Personality and Social Psychology*, Vol.30: 144–9.

Charlton, T. (1992) 'Giving access to the National Curriculum by working on the "self"', in Jones, K. and Charlton, T. (eds), *Learning Difficulties in Primary Classrooms: Delivering the Whole Curriculum*, London: Routledge.

Chazan, M., Laing, A.F., Bailey, M.S. and Jones, G. (1980) *Some of Our Children*, London: Open Books.

Clay, M.M. (1972) *The Early Detection of Reading Difficulties; A Diagnostic Survey*, London: Heinemann Educational Books.

Connor, M. (1994) 'Specific difficulty (dyslexia) and interventions', *Support for Learning*, Vol. 9, No. 3, August: 114–19.

Critchley, M. and Critchley, E.A. (1978) *Dyslexia Defined*, London: Heinemann.

Croll, P. and Moses, D. (1985) *One in Five*, London: Routledge and Kegan Paul.

Denton, C. and Postlethwaite, K. (1985) *Able Children: Identifying Them in the Classroom*, Windsor: NFER-Nelson.

Department for Education (1993) *Education Act, Chapter 35*, London: HMSO.

—— (1994a) Circular 6/94, *The Organisation of Special Educational Provision*, London: DFE.

—— (1994b) Circular 9/94, *The Education of Children with Emotional and Behavioural Difficulties*, London: DFE.

—— (1994c) *Code of Practice on the Identification and Assessment of Special Educational Needs*, London: Central Office of Information.

—— (1994d) *The Education (Special Educational Needs) (Information) Regulations 1994*, Statutory Instrument No. 1048, London: DFE.

Department of Education and Science (1978) *Special Educational Needs* (The Warnock Report), London: HMSO.

—— (1981) Education Act, London: HMSO.

—— (1983) *Circular 1/83 Assessments and Statements of Special Educational Needs* (Joint circular with the Department of Health and Social Services HC 83/3), London: DES and DHS.

—— Welsh Office (1989) *Discipline in Schools*, Report of the Committee of Enquiry chaired by Lord Elton, London: HMSO.

Dolton, R. (1991) 'Parents and professionals', in Tilstone, C. (ed.), *Teaching Pupils with Severe Learning Difficulties*, London: David Fulton.

Dunne, E. and Bennett, N. (1990) *Talking and Learning in Groups*, London: Macmillan Education.

Dyke, S. (1992) 'Providing for pupils' writing needs', in Jones, K. and Charlton, T. (eds), *Learning Difficulties in Primary Classrooms: Delivering the Whole Curriculum*, London: Routledge.

Dyson, A. (1991) 'Rethinking roles, rethinking concepts: special needs teachers in mainstream schools', *Support for Learning*, Vol. 6, No. 2, May: 51–60.

—— (1992) 'Innovatory mainstream practice: what's happening in schools' provision for special needs', *Support for Learning*, Vol. 7, No. 2, May: 51–7.

Evans, M. and Wilson, M. (1980) *Education of Disturbed Pupils*, Schools Council Working Paper 65, London: Methuen Educational.

Farnham-Diggory, S. (1992) *The Learning Disabled Child*, Cambridge, Mass.:, Harvard University Press.

Freeman, J. (1979) *Gifted Children*, Lancaster: MTP Press Ltd.

—— (1983) 'Identifying the able child', in Kerry, T. (eds), *Finding and Helping the Able Child*, London: Croom Helm.

Galloway, D. (1985) *Schools, Pupils and Special Educational Needs*, London: Croom Helm.

Galloway, D. and Goodwin, C. (1985) *The Education of Disturbing Children*, London: Longman.

Galton, M., Simon, B. and Croll, P. (1980) *Inside the Primary Classroom*, London: Routledge and Kegan Paul.

Goodlad, S. and Hirst, B. (1990) *Explorations in Peer Tutoring*, Oxford: Blackwell.

Greenhalgh, P. (1994) *Emotional Growth and Learning*, London: Routledge.

Gross, J. (1993) *Special Educational Needs in the Primary School: A Practical Guide*, Milton Keynes: Open University Press.

Hegarty, J.R. (1991) *The Present and Future of Microcomputers for People with Learning Difficulties*, Market Drayton: Change Publications.

Hegarty, S., Pocklington, K. and Lucas, D. (1981) *Educating Pupils with Special Needs in the Ordinary School*, Windsor: NFER-Nelson.

Heller, C. (1994) 'Closing the gap: compensating for literacy delay in children with specific learning difficulties/dyslexia', *Support for Learning* ,Vol. 9, No. 4, November: 162–5.

Hornsby, B. and Shear, F. (1975) *Alpha to Omega: The A–Z of Teaching Reading, Writing and Spelling*, London: Heinemann Educational Books.

Howarth, S.B. (1987) *Effective Integration: Physically Handicapped Children in Primary Schools*, Windsor: NFER-Nelson.

Hoyle, E. and Wilks, J. (1974) *Gifted Children and their Education*, London:

Department of Education and Science.

Jamieson, M., Parlett, M. and Pocklington, K. (1977) *Towards Integration: A Study of Blind and Partially Sighted Children in Ordinary Schools*, Slough: NFER.

Kerry, T. (ed.) (1983) *Finding and Helping the Able Child*, London: Croom Helm.

Knapman, D. (1985) 'The Elmwood Project, Somerset', in Topping, K. and Wolfendale, S. (eds), *Parental Involvement in Children's Reading*, London: Croom Helm.

Kounin, J. (1970) *Discipline and Group Management in Classrooms*, New York: Holt, Rinehart and Winston.

Lacy, P. (1991) 'Managing the classroom environment', in Tilstone, C. (ed.), *Teaching Pupils with Severe Learning Difficulties*, London: David Fulton.

Lewis, A. (1991) *Primary Special Needs and the National Curriculum*, London: Routledge.

Leyden, S. (1985) *Helping the Child of Exceptional Ability*, London: Croom Helm.

Lowenfeld, B. (1974) *The Visually Handicapped Child in School*, London: Constable.

Lyons, W. (1986) *Integrating the Handicapped in Ordinary Schools*, London: Croom Helm.

McConachie, H. (1986) *Parents and Young Handicapped Children: A Review of Research Issues*, London: Croom Helm.

Maltby, F. (1984) *Gifted Children and Teachers in the Primary School 5–12*, London: Falmer.

Marjoram, T. (1988) *Teaching Able Children*, London: Kogan Page.

Mittler, P. (1990) 'Foreword: Towards education for all', in Montgomery, D., *Special Needs in Ordinary Schools: Children with Learning Difficulties*, London: Cassell.

Mittler, P. and Mittler, H. (1982) *Partnership with Parents*, Stratford: National Council for Special Education.

Montgomery, D. (1990) *Special Needs in Ordinary Schools: Children with Learning Difficulties*, London: Cassell.

Moses, D. (1982) 'Special educational needs: the relationship between teacher assessment, test scores and classroom behaviour', *British Educational Research Journal*, Vol. 8, No. 2.

National Curriculum Council (1989) *A Curriculum for All: Special Educational Needs in the National Curriculum, Curriculum Guidance 2*, York: NCC.

O'Connor, M. (1994) 'Kindly take your seats', *Times Educational Supplement* , 21 October: 3.

Ogilvie, E. (1973) *Gifted Children in Primary Schools*, London: Macmillan.

Pearson, L. and Lindsay, G. (1986) *Special Needs in the Primary School: Identification and Intervention*, Windsor: NFER-Nelson.

Postlethwaite, K. and Hackney, A. (1988) *Organising a School's Response: Special Needs in Mainstream Schools*, London and Basingstoke: Macmillan.

Pyke, N. (1995) 'Emerging from the shadow of disability', *Times Educational Supplement*, 17 March: 4.

Ramasut, A. (ed.) (1989) *Whole School Approaches to Special Needs*, London: Falmer.

Ricks, D.M. and Wing, L. (1976) 'Language, communication and the use of symbols', in Wing, L. (ed.), *Early Childhood Autism*, Oxford: Pergamon Press.

Sewell, D.F. (1991) 'The release of cognitive resources – what can enabling technology enable?', in Hegarty, J.R., *The Present and Future of Microcomputers for People with Learning Difficulties*, Market Drayton: Change Publications.

Spodek, B., Saracho, O.N. and Lee, B.C. (1983) *Mainstreaming Young Children*, Belmont, Calif.: Wadsworth Publishing Company.

Tanner, J.M. (1978) *Foetus into Man*, London: Open Books.

Tansley, P. and Panckhurst, J. (1981) *Children with Specific Learning Difficulties*, Windsor: NFER-Nelson

Taylor, J.E. (1976) 'The principles of remedial education for autistic children', in Wing, L. (ed.), *Early Childhood Autism*, Oxford: Pergamon Press

Tilstone, C. (ed.) (1991) *Teaching Pupils with Severe Learning Difficulties*, London: David Fulton.

Tingle, M. (1990) *The Motor Impaired Child*, Windsor: NFER-Nelson.

Tizard, B., Blatchford, P., Burke, J., Farquhar, C. and Lewis, I. (1988) *Young Children at School in the Inner City*, London: Lawrence Erlbaum Associates.

Topping, K.J. and Lindsay, G.A. (1992) 'Paired reading: a review of the literature', in *Research Papers in Education Policy and Practice*, Vol. 7, No. 3, October: 199–245.

Topping, K.J. and Wolfendale, S. (eds) (1985) *Parental Involvement in Children's Reading*, London: Croom Helm.

Wheldall, K. and Merritt, F. (1984a) *BATPACK*, Birmingham: Positive Products/University of Birmingham.

—— (1984b) *Positive Teaching: The Behavioural Approach*, London: Unwin Educational Books.

Wing, L. (ed.) (1976) *Early Childhood Autism*, Oxford: Pergamon Press.

Wolfendale, S. (ed.) (1992a) *Empowering Parents and Teachers: Working for Children*, London: Cassell Educational Ltd.

—— (1992b) *Primary Schools and Special Needs: Policy, Planning, Provision* (2nd edn), London: Cassell Educational Ltd.

Wolfendale, S. and Bryans, T. (1978) *Identification of Learning Difficulties*, Stafford: National Association for Remedial Education.

Wood, D., Wood, H., Griffiths, A. and Howarth, I. (1986) *Teaching and Talking with Deaf Children*, John Wiley: Chichester.

Wright, A. (1994) 'Evaluation of Reading Recovery in Surrey: a reply to Kathleen Hall', *British Educational Research Journal*, Vol. 20, No. 1: 129–368.

Young, P. and Tye, C. (1992) *Gifted or Able: Realising Children's Potential*, Milton Keynes: Open University Press.

Index